The Famous Five and You
Search for Treasure!

1

Join the Famous Five on their wonderful
adventure to the ruined castle on Kirrin
Island. Find the submerged wreck and face
capture by ruthless gold hunters. *You* can
choose a pathway for the Five to the
treasure – but can you go straight to the
gold or will you be held up taking a false
trail on the way?

This exciting game story is based on Enid
Blyton's *Five on a Treasure Island*.

Join the action in
The Famous Five and You!

Enid Blyton, who died in 1968 at the age of 71 became, during her lifetime, Britain's best-loved and most popular author, and is still considered to have wielded a greater influence than any other author over children's writing in the post-war years. She loved young people, and wrote for 'all children, any children, everywhere' – over 600 books, many songs, poems and plays.

THE FAMOUS FIVE & YOU ①

SEARCH FOR TREASURE!

An Enid Blyton story
devised and adapted by
Mary Danby

Based on Enid Blyton's
Five on a Treasure Island

Illustrated by Trevor Parkin

KNIGHT BOOKS
Hodder and Stoughton

Text copyright © 1987 Mary
Danby/Darrell Waters Limited
Illustrations copyright © 1987
Hodder and Stoughton Limited

*First published in Great Britain in
1987 by Knight Books*

Enid Blyton is a Trade Mark of
Darrell Waters Limited

British Library C.I.P.

Danby, Mary
   Search for treasure! – (The
   Famous five and you; 1).
   1. Adventure games – Juvenile
   literature
   I. Title   II. Parkin, Trevor
   III. Blyton, Enid. Five on a
   treasure island
   IV. Series
   793′.9   GV1203

   ISBN 0-340-41100-7

Printed and bound in Great Britain
for Hodder and Stoughton
Paperbacks, a division of Hodder
and Stoughton Limited, Mill Road,
Dunton Green, Sevenoaks, Kent.
TN13 2YA. (Editorial Office:
47 Bedford Square, London
WC1B 3DP) by Cox & Wyman
Limited, Reading, Berks

Photoset by Rowland
Phototypesetting Limited,
Bury St Edmunds, Suffolk

THE FAMOUS FIVE AND YOU

Unlike an ordinary book, which you can read straight through from beginning to end, this is a game book, in which *you* choose how the story should go.

Begin at paragraph number 1. When you have read it, you'll see that you can choose what happens next. If you think the family should travel by car, you turn to paragraph 6; if you think they should travel by train, you go to paragraph 4.

Every time you have a choice to make, there will be one way that is the quickest and best – and you have to guess (or work out, if you can) which it is. If you choose the wrong paragraph, you can still carry on reading, but when you find yourself back at the main story you will find you have picked up a few 'red herrings'.

A red herring is the name given to something that carries you away from the main subject (as when someone tells you a story and puts in all sorts of details that don't really matter). Your aim is to try to stay on the main track without going off down the side roads.

See if you can make the right choices and find your way to the end of the story without picking up too many red herrings. Red herrings are represented in the text by a symbol: ◯◁. (Use a pencil and paper to add up your score as you go along.) Then turn to the back of the book to see how well the Famous Five (and You) have done.

1

'This holidays Daddy wants me to go to Scotland with him,' said Mother to Julian, Dick and Anne. 'We thought it would be fun for you to have a holiday on your own, but I don't really know where to send you.'

'They could go to Quentin's,' said Daddy. Quentin was the children's uncle. He was a stern man, a scientist who spent his time studying. He and his wife Fanny lived by the sea, at Kirrin Bay.

'Is Kirrin Bay nice?' asked Anne. 'Are there cliffs and rocks and sand?'

'I don't remember it very well,' said Daddy, 'but I feel sure it's an exciting kind of place.'

'They have a daughter called Georgina,' said Mother. 'You three would be company for her.'

'Oh Daddy, do telephone Aunt Fanny and ask her if we can go,' said Dick. 'It sounds sort of adventurous!'

Daddy rang Aunt Fanny and settled everything. 'You can go next week, but you must promise not to disturb Uncle Quentin. He's working very hard.'

'Are we going by train or car?' asked Dick.

If you think that they should go by train, go to **4**. *If you think that they should go by car, go to* **6**.

2

'Well, we did have breakfast very early,' said Mother. 'Perhaps we could stop soon. You children look for a good spot.'

In a little while Dick saw a field with a little stream running through it. They had a huge lunch, and then the children had a quick paddle in the stream before they got back in the car.

After they had been going about ten minutes, Anne gave a cry: 'Oh, gosh!'

Go to **12**.

3

If you have arrived from **12**, *score* ◯↰

After several hours in the car they reached a signpost that said: 'Kirrin Bay 2 miles'.

The children began to feel excited.

'We must watch out for the sea,' said Dick. 'I can smell it somewhere near!'

The car suddenly topped a hill – and there was the shining blue sea, calm and smooth in the evening sun.

'We've made good time,' said Daddy. 'You'll see the bay soon, with a funny sort of island at its entrance.'

'There it is – that must be Kirrin Bay!' shouted Julian.

'And look at the rocky little island guarding the entrance,' said Dick. 'I'd like to visit that.'

'Here's Kirrin Cottage,' said Daddy. He stopped the car in front of a big house built of old white stone with roses climbing over the front of it.

'Now – where's Quentin? Hello, there's Fanny.'

Go to **5**.

4

'Let's go by train,' said Daddy. 'Mother and I will come down with you. If we get there at tea-time, we'll be able to have tea with Quentin and Fanny and catch a train back in the evening. I'll ring the station and check the times of trains.'

But when he got through to the station he discovered that there was only one train to Kirrin Bay each day, and it didn't arrive until late in the evening.

'Bother,' said Julian. 'Oh well, what shall we do?'

Go to **6**.

5

The children liked the look of Aunt Fanny at once.

'Welcome to Kirrin!' she cried. 'It's lovely to see you!'

They all went into the house. It felt old and

rather mysterious, somehow. The furniture was very beautiful.

'Where's Georgina?' asked Anne.

'She's gone off somewhere, the naughty girl,' said Aunt Fanny. 'I must tell you, children, you may find George a bit difficult – she's always been one on her own. At first she may not like you being here, but I think she badly needs other children to play with.'

'Why do you call her "George"?' asked Anne.

'She hates being a girl,' replied her aunt, 'so we have to call her George, as if she were a boy. The naughty girl won't answer if we call her Georgina.'

Go to **11**.

6

If you have arrived from **4**, *score one red herring:* . *If not, well done – you went the right way!*

'Let's go by car,' said Mother.

'Right,' said Daddy. 'We can pile everything into the boot. We'll go on Tuesday, shall we?'

The children counted the days eagerly, but the week seemed very long. At last Tuesday came, and they set off after breakfast. Mother sat in front with Daddy, and the three children sat behind.

Along the crowded London roads they went until they found themselves out in the open countryside.

'Are we picnicking soon?' asked Anne, feeling hungry all of a sudden.

'Yes,' said Mother. 'But not yet. It's only eleven o'clock. We shan't have lunch until at least half-past twelve.'

'Gracious!' said Anne. 'I know I can't last out until then!'

If you think they should stop and have their picnic now, go to **2**. *If you think they should wait until later, go to* **10**.

7

They were very excited at the possibility of meeting their mysterious cousin, and ran down to where the girl was paddling.

'Hello,' said Julian. 'I'm Julian. Are you our cousin Georgina?'

'No,' said the strange girl. 'My name is Sarah, and I'm on holiday here.'

Go to **19**.

8

But it was no good. The yawn escaped, and both the boys scowled at her because they knew what would happen next. And it did!

'Poor Anne! How tired you are. You must all go to bed straight away and have a good long night,' said Aunt Fanny.

'Anne, you *are* an idiot,' said Dick. 'I wanted to go down to the beach for a while.'

'I'm sorry,' said Anne. 'And anyway, *you're* yawning now, Dick – and Julian too!'

Go to **13**.

9

After a minute she managed to swallow her yawn.

'Now,' said Aunt Fanny. 'Would you like to go down to the beach for a while before bed-time?'

'Oh yes, please,' said the children. They had all secretly been hoping Aunt Fanny would say this.

'Well, it's not far,' said their aunt. 'Follow the path at the left of the front gate and it will take you straight there.'

The children rushed off.

Go to **20**.

10

Mother handed them all some chocolate, and they munched it happily until it was time for lunch. The picnic was lovely. They had it on top of a hill, looking down into a sunny valley. The children ate enormously.

'What time shall we be at Aunt Fanny's?' asked Julian.

'About six o'clock, with luck,' said Daddy.

Go to **3**.

Uncle Quentin suddenly appeared. He was very tall and dark, with a rather fierce frown.

'Hello, Quentin,' said Daddy. 'I hope these three won't disturb you too much in your work.'

Their uncle nodded to the three children. The frown didn't come off his face, and they all felt a little scared.

There was no room for Mother and Daddy to stay the night, so after a hurried supper they said goodbye to the children and left to stay at a hotel, from where they would drive straight back to London the next morning. They sent their love to Georgina, who still hadn't appeared.

Anne suddenly felt tired, and struggled not to yawn.

If you think Anne manages not to yawn, go to **9**. *If she yawns, go to* **8**.

'What's the matter?' asked her mother.

'I've left my socks beside the stream where we picnicked,' said Anne.

'Well, you are a silly girl,' said Daddy crossly. 'Now we'll have to go back for them.'

He turned the car around and they hurried back to the picnic place. Having found Anne's socks, they continued on their journey.

'You are a pest, Anne,' said Dick. 'Now I expect we'll be late.'

Go to **3**.

13

If you have arrived from **25**, *score* ⊃⊄ ⊃⊄. *If you have arrived from* **19**, *score* ⊃⊄ ⊃⊄ ⊃⊄.

They were all fast asleep before Georgina came to bed. They were so tired that they heard nothing at all until the sun woke them in the morning.

When Anne woke up she looked across at the other bed. In it lay the figure of another child. Anne could just see the top of a curly head, and that was all. When the figure stirred a little, Anne spoke.

'I say, are you Georgina?'

The child in the opposite bed sat up and looked at Anne. Her hair was very short, and her blue eyes were bright against her sun-browned face. Her mouth was sulky, and she was frowning.

'No,' she said, 'I'm not Georgina.'

'Oh!' said Anne in surprise. 'Then who are you?'

'I'm George,' said the girl. 'I hate being a girl. You're to call me George. Then I'll speak to you. But I shan't if you don't.'

'Oh!' said Anne again. 'All right. Anyway, you look like a boy.'

'Don't you simply hate being a girl?' asked George.

14

'No,' said Anne. 'You see – I do like pretty dresses.'

'Fancy bothering about pretty dresses,' said George in a scornful voice. 'Well, you *are* a baby.'

Go to **17**.

14

But the sight of the blue sea stopped her feeling cross, and suddenly she thought it was rather unkind of her to leave her cousins alone on their first morning. She was not an unkind girl, just not used to considering others. As she turned to go back to the cottage, she saw her cousins coming along the beach and ran to join them.

Go to **30**.

15

'You must take your cousins out this morning, George,' said Aunt Fanny at breakfast. 'You can show them the best places to swim.'

'I'm going fishing,' said George.

'You are not,' said her father.

If you think George disobeys her father, go to **23**. *If not, go to* **21**.

16

'I bet I could,' said Dick. 'It looks jolly near to me.'

George scowled at him. 'You can't wade out there. The water's too deep!'

'Well, I'm going to have a go,' said Dick, and he ran off down the beach.

Go to **27**.

17

Anne felt offended. 'You won't find my brothers take much notice of you if you act as if you knew everything.'

'Well, if they're going to be nasty to me, I shan't take any notice of *them*,' said George. 'I'm quite happy on my own.'

They both got dressed in silence, then the boys hammered on their door.

'Cousin Georgina, come out and see us.'

George marched out, taking no notice of the two surprised boys.

'She won't answer if you call her Georgina,' explained Anne. 'She's awfully odd, I think.'

They all ran down to breakfast.

Go to **15**.

18

The three children stared at George.

'I'll tell you how Kirrin Island belongs to me,' she said. 'Years ago my mother's family owned all the land around here, but all that's left is our house and Kirrin Island. Mother says she doesn't want it now, so she's sort of given it to me.'

The four children looked out over the bay to the island. The tide was going out.

'I'm going to wade over to the island,' declared Dick, kicking off his shoes.

'I shouldn't try, if I were you,' said George.

Should Dick try to wade to the island? If so, go to **16**. *If not, go to* **22**.

19

The children were disappointed that it was not Georgina, and soon afterwards went back to the cottage. By now they were all very sleepy.

Go to **13**.

They ran down the path and soon came to a wide sandy beach.

'What a pity we didn't bring our swimming things,' said Dick.

'Never mind,' said Julian. 'We can swim tomorrow.'

Anne suddenly pointed to a girl who was walking by the sea.

'Look,' she said. 'Do you think that's Georgina?'

'It might be,' said Julian. 'Shall we go and ask her who she is?'

If you think they should, go to **7**. *If not, go to* **25**.

21

'You are going to show a few good manners for a change, and take your cousins to the bay,' said Uncle Quentin. 'Do you hear me?'

'Yes,' said George, scowling.

So after breakfast the four children made their way down to the beach.

Go to **30**.

22

If you have arrived from **27**, *score* ⌒⌒.

'It's only possible to get to the island by boat,'

George went on. 'It's further out than it looks, and the water is very, very deep, and there are a lot of wrecks about.'

'Wrecks!' cried Julian, his eyes shining. 'Are there any to see?'

'Only one now,' said George, 'and that's on the other side of the island. The wreck really belongs to me too.'

The children could hardly believe George.

'Yes,' she said, 'it was a ship belonging to my great-great-great-grandfather. He was bringing big bars of gold back in his ship, and it got wrecked off Kirrin Island. Nobody knows what happened to the gold.'

'Golly – this does sound exciting!' said Julian.

Go to **28**.

23

George got down from the table and rushed out.

'George!' shouted Uncle Quentin. 'Come back!'

But George was already running down the beach path.

'It's horrid having three cousins to look after,' she said to herself. 'I'm quite happy on my own. I jolly well won't take them to see the bay, whatever Mother and Father say.'

Go to **14**.

They saw a big black and white mongrel with an absurdly long tail and a big wide mouth that really seemed to grin! George came running down to them.

'This is Timmy,' she said. 'Don't you think he's simply perfect?'

He was such a friendly, clumsy, laughable creature that all the children adored him at once.

'Is he yours? Why doesn't he live with you?' asked Anne.

George's face had gone sulky again. 'Father said Timmy's bark nearly drove him mad, so he hit Timmy. That made me angry, and I was rude to Father. So he said I couldn't keep Timmy any more.'

'What did you do?' asked Julian.

'I went to Alf, the son of a fisherman I know,' said George, 'and asked him to keep Timmy for me. I pay him all the pocket money I get. That's why I never have any money to spend. You must all promise never to tell anyone at home that I'm still keeping Timmy.'

'We promise!' cried the children.

'You're nice,' said George. 'I'm glad you've come, after all. Let's take a boat out this afternoon and row around the island to look at the wreck, shall we?'

'Rather!' said all three at once – and even Timmy wagged his tail as if he understood.

Go to **29**.

'No,' said Dick, 'I'm sure it's not Georgina. That girl has fair hair, and Georgina is dark. Aunt Fanny showed me a picture of her.'

After exploring the beach for a while they went back to the cottage. By now they were all very sleepy.

Go to **13**.

Anne was just about to say that they liked Timmy too when she got such a kick on her ankle that she cried out in pain. George glared at her.

'George! Why did you kick Anne?' cried Aunt Fanny. 'Leave the table at once! I won't have such behaviour.'

George left the table without a word. She went out to the garden.

'I expect she'll go into the sulks now,' said her mother. 'Dear, dear, she's *such* a difficult child!'

The children didn't mind George going into the sulks. What they did mind was that George might refuse to take them to see the wreck now!

They finished their meal in silence, then Anne went into the garden to find George. She was lying on her back under a big tree.

'I'm sorry I nearly made a mistake, George,' said Anne.

George sat up. 'I've a good mind not to take you to see the wreck,' she said. 'Stupid baby!'

Anne's heart sank. 'Oh please do,' she said.

Will George forgive Anne? If she does, go to **41**. *If not, go to* **36**.

27

The others watched as Dick started to wade into the water. He hadn't gone very far when he suddenly found himself in water that reached his waist. He took a few more steps, but soon found he could hardly keep his head above water, so he turned and waded out. Soon he was back with the others.

'Gosh,' said Julian. 'Aunt Fanny will be cross with you. Your shirt and shorts are soaking.'

'It's a lovely hot day,' said Anne. 'Dick's clothes will soon dry.'

George looked crossly at Dick. 'Now do you believe me?' she said coldly.

Go to **22**.

28

'I say, George – what about a swim?' said Dick.

'I must go and get Timmy first,' said George, and she run off up the cliff path.

'Who in the world can Timmy be?' wondered Julian.

The children lay back on the soft sand and waited. Soon they heard George's voice coming down the cliff behind them.

'Come on, Timmy! Come on!'

They sat up to see what Timmy was like.

Go to **24**.

29

By lunchtime they were all very hungry. They went back up the cliff path hoping there would be lots to eat – and there was!

'What are you going to do this afternoon?' asked George's mother.

'George is going to take us to see the wreck on the other side of the island,' said Anne.

'*George* is going to take you!' said Aunt Fanny. 'Why, George – what's come over you? You've never taken a single person before, though I've asked you dozens of times.'

George shook her head. 'I'm not doing it because you asked me. I'm doing it because I want to. I like them.'

Her mother laughed. 'Well, it's good news that you like your cousins,' she said. 'I hope they like you.'

'Oh yes!' said Anne eagerly. 'We do like George – and we like Ti . . .'

Go to **26**.

If you have arrived from **14**, *score* ⌒⊃.

Anne stared out over the bay. At the entrance to it lay the curious rocky island with what looked like an old ruined castle on the top of it.

'Isn't that a funny place?' she said. 'I wonder what it's called.'

'It's called Kirrin Island,' said George. 'I may take you there some day.'

'Who does the island belong to?' asked Julian.

George made a most surprising answer. 'It belongs to *me*,' she said.

Go to **18**.

31

If you have arrived from **46**, *score* ⌒⊃ ⌒⊃. *If you have arrived from* **33**, *score* ⌒⊃ ⌒⊃ ⌒⊃.

Alf, a brown-faced boy of about fourteen, had the boat all ready, down on the beach. Now that George had recovered from her sulks she was in high spirits, grinning at her cousins and throwing stones into the sea for Timmy to splash after.

They all jumped into the boat, including Timmy, who sprayed them with cold water every time he wagged his big tail. George rowed splendidly, and the boat shot along over the blue bay.

'I say, we're getting near your island now,' said Julian. 'It's bigger than I thought. Isn't the castle exciting?'

They drew close to the island.

Go to **37**.

32

'I'll stay with Anne,' said Dick.

'Thanks, Dick,' said Julian. 'You keep the boat round about here.'

George and Julian stripped off their jeans and jerseys, and then George took a beautiful header off the end of the boat. The others watched her swimming strongly downwards.

After a while she came up, bursting for breath.

'I wish I could get right into the ship,' she said. 'But I never have enough breath for that. You go down now, Julian.'

Julian was not as good at swimming under water as George was, and he couldn't go down so far, but he was able to have a good look at the deck of the ship, which looked forlorn and strange. He was glad to get to the surface of the water again and take deep breaths of air.

He climbed into the boat.

'Most exciting,' he said. 'Golly, wouldn't I just love to see that wreck properly! Perhaps we could find the lost gold.'

'That's impossible,' said George. 'Proper divers have already gone down and found nothing.

What's the time? I say, we'll be late for tea if we don't hurry back now!'

Go to **45**.

33

'Hello! Is anyone there?' said the voice. 'Who are you?'

The next moment a man appeared in the doorway. He wore rough country clothes and had a dark red scar across his cheek.

'What are you children doing here?' he said angrily. 'Don't you know that this is private property? Go away, before I call the police!'

'I'm very sorry,' said Julian. 'We didn't know we weren't allowed in. We'll go at once.'

The children walked back along the cliff path. Below them they could see the beach and the bay, sparkling in the sun.

'Look,' said Anne, who had very keen sight. 'Isn't that George and Timmy, down by the boat? Perhaps she's stopped sulking now. Let's go and see.'

They ran down to join them.

Go to **31**.

34

If you have arrived from **42**, *score* ◁.

'I promised we'd be back for tea,' said George. 'I

don't think we can land today if we want to see the wreck as well. We'll come back another day and land on the island.'

George rowed steadily out a little beyond the island. Then she stopped and looked back to the shore.

'How do you know when you are over the wreck?' asked Julian, puzzled.

'Well, do you see that church tower on the mainland?' asked George. 'When you get it exactly in line with the top of that hill over there, you are pretty well over the wreck.'

Go to **49**.

35

The children's aunt arranged a picnic for them the next day, and they all went to a little cove not far off where they could bathe and paddle to their hearts' content.

George didn't want to go, because her mother was going on the picnic too, which meant that George had to pass a whole day without her beloved Timmy.

Go to **52**.

36

'No,' said George. 'Now go away and leave me alone.'

Anne went back to the house, trying not to cry.

'It's no good,' she said to the boys. 'George is awfully cross with me for nearly giving away the secret of Timmy, and she won't take any of us to the island.'

'Oh well,' said Julian, 'we'll just have to find something else to do. Have either of you two got any ideas?'

'I know,' cried Dick. 'Let's explore the cliffs on the other side of Kirrin Cottage.'

'Or we could go and find Alf,' suggested Anne, 'and ask him if we can take Timmy for a walk.'

If you think they should explore the cliffs, go to **39**. *If you think they should go and find Alf, go to* **40**.

37

In the very middle of the island rose the castle. It had been built of big white stones, but now ruined walls were all that were left.

'It looks awfully mysterious,' said Julian. 'Wouldn't it be fun to spend a night here!'

'Oh yes, rather,' said Dick. 'Do you think your mother would let us?'

'I don't know,' said George. 'She might. You could ask her.'

'Can we land there this afternoon, George?' asked Julian.

If George says yes, go to **42**. *If she says no, go to* **34**.

If you have arrived from **54**, *score* ⬡.

'I think there's going to be a storm,' said George, looking out towards the south-west. 'See the little white tops to the waves? That's always a bad sign.'

'Oh George – it will be the biggest disappointment of our lives if we don't go today. Oh please, can we go?' said Anne. 'And besides,' she added artfully, 'if we hang about the house we won't be able to have Timmy with us.'

'Well . . . all right, then, we'll go,' said George. 'But if a storm does come, you're not to be a baby.'

'Don't worry, Anne, I'll look after you,' said Julian.

Go to **48**

39

'I'd rather like to investigate those cliffs,' said Julian. 'There's a funny old tumbledown house I can see out of our bedroom window. It looks jolly mysterious.'

'Yes, it does,' agreed Dick. 'Come on, Anne. You can see Timmy later.'

Soon the three children were following the cliff path. The cliffs were very steep and Anne felt rather frightened, but she didn't tell Julian and Dick. She didn't want them to think she was a baby.

Go to **43**.

'I don't see why we should take George's dog for a walk when she's so rotten to Anne,' said Dick.

'Well, it's not Timmy's fault that George is in the sulks,' said Julian. 'Maybe she'll feel better if she finds out we've been kind to Timmy.' So off they ran to find Alf.

Go to **46**.

41

'Even if you don't take me,' Anne went on, 'you might take the boys. After all, they didn't do anything silly. And anyway, look at the bruise I've got.'

George looked at it. 'But wouldn't you be miserable if I took Julian and Dick without you?'

'Of course,' said Anne, 'but I don't want them to miss a treat.'

Then George did a surprising thing. She gave Anne a hug. 'It's all right,' she said gruffly. 'Of course you can come.'

Go to **31**.

42

'Oh yes, do let's,' said Anne. 'I'm longing to see the castle!'

'All right, then,' said George, starting to row. Suddenly the sea seemed rougher than when they had set out.

'Golly,' said George. 'I think the wind must have changed direction.'

'I know!' said Julian. 'If I use my watch as a compass I can tell which direction the wind is blowing from.'

Anne peered over his shoulder. 'I didn't know you could use a watch as a compass,' she said.

'Oh, it's simple,' said Julian. 'You just point the hour hand at the sun, and a line drawn between that and twelve o'clock would point north–south. Goodness, look at the time! It's nearly four o'clock!'

Go to **34**.

43

Soon they reached the tumbledown house. It was a very strange and ghostly-looking kind of place.

'Do you suppose a smuggler lived here?' said Dick. 'Perhaps there is a secret hiding-place where he hid his smuggled jewels.'

'Perhaps the gold from the wreck was brought here,' said Julian excitedly. 'Let's search for a hiding-place.'

They peered all around the outside of the cottage, tapping the walls and feeling into crevices, but couldn't find anything that might have been a hiding-place.

The front door was hanging open. 'I don't suppose anyone would mind if we took a look inside,' said Julian. 'After all, nobody lives here.'

One by one they explored all the rooms on the ground floor, but they found nothing. They were just about to test the stairs to see if they were safe when they heard a voice outside.

Go to **33**.

44

'You don't sound at all as if you want me to,' said George's mother in a hurt tone. 'No, I shan't come tomorrow, but I'm sure your cousins must think you are an odd girl never to want your mother to go with you.'

George said nothing. Neither did the others. They knew perfectly well that it wasn't that George didn't want her mother to go – it was just that she wanted Timmy with her.

'Anyway, I couldn't come,' went on Aunt Fanny. 'I've got some gardening to do.'

Next day the sun was shining, and everything seemed splendid.

'Isn't it a marvellous day,' Anne said to George as they sat down to breakfast. 'I'm so looking forward to going to the island.'

'Well, honestly, I'm not sure we ought to go,' said George unexpectedly.

'Oh, but why?' cried Anne in dismay.

Go to **38**.

45

If you have arrived from **60**, score ⌒ ⌒.

They were only about five minutes late, and after tea they went out for a walk over the moors with Timmy at their heels. By the time bedtime came they were all so sleepy that they could hardly keep their eyes open.

'Goodnight, George,' said Anne, snuggling down into her bed. 'We've had a lovely day – thanks to you!'

'And *I've* had a lovely day too,' said George, rather gruffly. 'Thanks to *you*.'

Go to **35**.

46

George, alone in the garden, heard them go and felt very unhappy. She hadn't meant to hurt Anne, but she loved Timmy so much she was afraid that if her parents found out that Alf was looking after Timmy they would take the dog away and sell him.

Somehow, though, she couldn't stay cross when she thought about how nice her cousins were. She got up and ran down to the beach, taking a short cut, so she arrived before them.

Go to **31**.

47

'You stay with Anne, Julian,' said Dick. 'I'm going to dive down to the wreck.'

'You won't be able to dive right down to it,' said George. 'It's too far down. I can hold my breath for a long time under water, but I've never been able to get right down to the wreck.'

'I bet *I* can,' said Dick.

George scowled at him. 'You can try if you like,' she said. 'But I bet you jolly well can't.'

Dick stood up, making the boat rock. 'Change places with me, Anne,' he said. 'Then I can dive off the bow.'

Anne stood up and started to move down the boat. Just then, a powerful motor-boat appeared from behind the headland and roared past them. George's boat rocked violently in the wash. Anne gave a shriek, and fell into the water!

Go to **53**.

48

Aunt Fanny made sandwiches for them, and they set off at last with the food in two kit-bags. The first thing they did was to fetch Timmy from Alf's yard, then they all made their way to the beach.

'You won't be very long, will you?' called Alf as he pushed the boat off. 'There's a storm blowing up. Bad one it'll be, too.'

Go to **57**.

49

She stopped rowing. They all looked eagerly over the sides of the boat to see if they could spy the wreck in the water. Suddenly they saw something deep down!

'It's the wreck!' said Julian. 'I can see a bit of broken mast. Look, Dick, look! Gosh, I wish I could dive down and get a closer look at it!'

'Well, why don't you?' said George.

'Can I go down too?' asked Dick.

'I'm going to dive down first, as it's *my* wreck,' said George. 'But one of you two boys will have to stay in the boat with Anne. Which one of you is it going to be?'

Who should stay in the boat? If it is Dick, go to **32**. *If it is Julian, go to* **47**.

50

If you have arrived from **55**, *score* ◁ ◁.

The others persuaded George that they should explore the castle right away.

'Look,' said George. 'That's where the entrance used to be – through that big broken archway.' She pointed upwards. 'See those two towers? One is nearly gone, but jackdaws live in the other one. They've almost filled it up with their sticks.'

They went through a ruined doorway into what looked like a great yard. Its stone floor was now overgrown with weeds.

'This is the centre of the castle,' said George. 'Here is where the people used to live. You can see where the rooms were. Look – there's one that's

almost whole. Go through that little door and you'll see it.'

Go to **63**.

51

I really must see what the waves are like, thought Julian. He climbed up on to part of the ruined castle wall and looked out to sea. What a sight met his eyes!

The waves were like great walls of grey-green. They rolled up to the island and dashed themselves against it with terrific force. He stared at the great waves coming in – and then he saw something strange.

There was something else out on the sea by the rocks besides the waves – something dark, something big, something that seemed to lurch out of the waves and settle down again. What could it be?

'It can't be a ship,' said Julian to himself. 'And yet it looks more like a ship than anything else. I wonder if I should try to get a closer look, or go and tell the others?'

If you think Julian should go closer, go to **61**. *If you think he should go back to the others, go to* **64**.

52

'What about going to my island tomorrow?' George asked Julian on the way home.

'Golly,' said Julian, his eyes shining. 'That would be marvellous. Come on, let's tell the others!'

As the children washed before supper they talked eagerly about the visit to the island the next day. Their aunt heard them and smiled.

'How about having lunch there, and spending the whole day?' she asked.

George looked up. 'Are you coming too, Mother?' she asked.

If Aunt Fanny says yes, go to **58**. *If she says no, go to* **44**.

Anne wasn't a strong swimmer like George, and she was in deep water. She rose to the surface, gasping and splashing. 'Julian!' she shrieked. 'Help me!'

In a flash Julian had dived into the water, and with a few strong strokes had reached his sister. Catching her firmly under her arms, he pulled her back to the boat.

George and Dick hauled Anne into the boat.

'Take your jeans and jersey off,' said George. 'You've got your swimsuit on underneath, and your clothes will soon dry in the sun.'

'What's the time?' asked Julian. 'I say, we'll be late for tea if we don't hurry back now.'

George started to row, and the boat moved smoothly over the calm sea.

'G . . . golly,' said Anne, her teeth chattering. 'I've just realised something. The m . . . man in the m . . . motor-boat was the same man who we saw at the t . . . tumbledown house!'

Go to **60**.

Go to **60**.

54

The children looked eagerly at the weather the following day when they got up. The sun was shining, and everything seemed splendid. They all ran down to have breakfast.

Aunt Fanny looked out of the window.

'It's a lovely day,' she said. 'I've got so much gardening to do that I think I'll stay at home and not come to the island with you.'

George's face lit up. Now she could take Timmy! Aunt Fanny noticed her smiling.

'Really, George,' she said, 'you look so pleased that I'm not coming with you that I'm sure your cousins will think you are very strange.'

George said nothing as she finished her breakfast. Then she got down from the table and went outside. In a little while the others joined her.

'You know, I'm not sure we ought to go to the island,' she said.

'Oh, but why?' cried Anne in dismay.

Go to **38**.

55

George showed them her favourite beach, which could be reached only by land as it was guarded by treacherous rocks, half covered by the sea. Anne found some lovely pink-striped shells, and Timmy dug a big hole in the sand.

It was a very small island, so it didn't take them long to explore the rest of it. After a while they went back to the boat to collect the food for lunch, and carried it up to the castle.

'Can we explore the castle now?' asked Dick.

'Oh please, George,' pleaded Anne.

Go to **50**.

'Thunder!' said George. 'That's the storm. It's coming sooner than I thought!'

'Let's have lunch,' said Dick, who was starving, as usual. 'Perhaps by the time we've finished the storm will be over.'

'Yes, we will in a minute,' said George. 'I say, just look at these big waves coming in! My word, it really *is* going to be a storm. Golly – what a flash of lightning!'

'Could we light a fire to make things a bit more cheerful?' asked Julian, looking around. 'There are plenty of sticks on the ground below the jackdaws' tower.'

He dashed out into the rain and picked up an armful of sticks.

'I've got some matches,' said George. Soon there was a fine, cracking fire going.

'I've never heard the sea making such an awful noise,' said Anne. 'It sounds as if it's shouting at the top of its voice.'

They finished their picnic, and Julian went to get more sticks.

Go to **51**.

Go to **51**.

57

George rowed all the way to the island, which looked even more exciting than it had the other day.

'Where are you going to land?' asked Julian. 'I simply can't imagine how you know your way in and out of these awful rocks.'

'I'm going to land at a little cove that's hidden away on the east side of the island,' said George.

As the boat rounded a low wall of sharp rocks, the children saw the cove she spoke of. It was like a little natural harbour – a smooth inlet of water running up to a beach. The boat slid into the inlet.

They landed on the smooth yellow sand, and George pulled the boat high out of the water.

'If a storm is coming,' she explained, 'we don't want to lose our boat.'

'Let's explore the island!' yelled Anne. 'Oh do come on!'

They all followed her. It really was a most exciting place. Rabbits were everywhere!

'Aren't they tame,' said Julian in surprise.

'Well, nobody ever comes here but me,' said George, 'and I don't frighten them.'

'There's the castle!' exclaimed Julian. 'Shall we explore that now? I do want to.'

'I think we should explore the island before the storm comes,' said George.

If you think they should explore the castle, go to **50**. *If you think they should explore the island, go to* **59**.

58

'Oh yes,' said Aunt Fanny. 'I haven't been over to the island for months. I'd like to visit it again.'

George scowled, and her cousins knew that she was cross at the idea of having to spend another day without Timmy. She said nothing, however, but she was very quiet until bedtime.

Go to **54**.

59

They decided to explore the island first.

'If we walk around the outside of the castle we may see the cormorants,' said George.

Sure enough, on the other side of the castle they saw some rocks sticking up, with great black shining birds sitting on them in awkward-looking positions.

'I think they've probably caught plenty of fish for their lunch, and they're sitting there digesting it. Come on — let's go down to the beach.'

Go to **55**.

60

'What tumbledown house?' asked George.

'The one up the cliff path from Kirrin Cottage,' said Julian. 'We went there after lunch, but a strange man appeared and told us to go away. He said it was private property.'

'It jolly well isn't,' said George. 'I've often

played in that old house. I wonder who he was, and what he was doing there.'

But there was no time to discuss it any further, and soon they were back at Kirrin Cottage for tea.

Go to **45**.

61

He decided to try to get a closer look at the mysterious dark shape, and set off towards it. The wind screamed in his ears, and the thunder crashed so loudly that it sounded almost as if mountains were falling down all around! He walked on to the rocks and at once found that he had trouble standing upright, they were so slippery and wet. All of a sudden his feet slipped from under him and he fell!

Go to **68**.

62

'Why don't we play cards?' suggested Dick. 'That should be quiet enough as long as we don't play Snap!'

The others all thought that this was a very good idea, and George went to find a pack of cards. They decided to play Beggar My Neighbour, and became so interested in the game that they didn't notice it was much later than usual when Aunt Fanny called them for supper.

'You were enjoying your game so much that I decided to get supper later, rather than stop you,' said Aunt Fanny.

As a result it was very late by the time they all got to bed, and they were all so sleepy that no one remembered that they had planned to get up early the following morning!

Go to **79**.

63

They trooped through a doorway and found themselves in a dark, stone-walled, stone-roofed room. Two slit-like windows lighted the room. It felt very mysterious.

'Were there any dungeons?' asked Dick.

'I don't know. I expect so,' said George. 'But they'd be very hard to find – everywhere is so overgrown.'

'Well, I think it's a perfectly lovely place,' said Anne.

'Golly,' said George, who was looking out of the side of the ruined castle, 'all the cormorants are flying away. I wonder why?'

She soon knew – from the south-west there suddenly came an ominous rumble.

Go to **56**.

64

If you have arrived from **68**, *score* ⌒ ⌒.

He hurried to where George, Dick and Anne were huddled by the fire. 'Listen, everyone! There's something odd out on the rocks beyond the island!' he shouted. 'It looks like a ship – yet it can't possibly be!'

The others stared at Julian in surprise, then jumped to their feet and followed him out into the rain.

Go to **66**.

65

'We couldn't possibly risk it now,' said George, 'while the waves are so big – and they won't go down today, that's certain. The wind is too strong.'

'Do you suppose people will still let you have it for your own now that the sea has thrown it up?' asked Dick. 'We'd better not tell anyone about it!'

'Don't be silly,' said George. 'One of the fishermen is sure to see it. The news will soon be out.'

'Well, we'll have to come early tomorrow,' said Julian. 'I'm sure lots of grown-ups will think it's their business to explore it too.'

Go to **70**.

The storm seemed to be passing over a little now. Julian led the way to the wall on which he had stood to watch the sea.

Everyone climbed up to gaze out to sea. At first they saw nothing, because the waves reared up too high. Then suddenly George saw what Julian meant. 'Gracious!' she shouted. 'It *is* a ship!'

The sea was bringing the ship nearer to shore.

'It will be dashed on to those rocks,' said Julian. 'Look – there it goes!'

As he spoke there came a tremendous crashing sound, and the dark shape of the ship settled down on to the sharp teeth of the rocks. It stayed there, shifting only slightly as the sea ran under it and lifted it a little.

Go to **72**.

It was pitch black when the torch went out, and Dick couldn't help feeling a bit frightened. In a minute, however, his eyes got used to the darkness and he could see a faint light coming from the hole up to the deck. Walking carefully across the seaweed he made his way over to the ladder and climbed up to the deck again.

'I'm afraid I've lost your torch, Julian,' he said. 'I dropped it down there and it went out.'

'Well, if we all go down together we may be able to find it,' said Julian. 'Come on.'

Go to **86**.

68

Julian managed to put out an arm to save himself from falling heavily, but he still caught his leg on a sharp rock and cut it.

'Bother!' he said to himself. He pulled out his handkerchief and tied it around his leg. By this time he was soaked through from the rain and the spray from the waves, and he decided that it would be sensible to go back to the others and tell them what he had seen. He got up and, walking very carefully over the slippery rocks, went back to the castle.

Go to **64**.

69

If you have arrived from **79**, *score* ⌒ ⌒.

Soon they were all creeping down the stairs to the front door.

The sun was shining brightly, and the day had a lovely new feeling about it. The sky was bright blue and the sea looked smooth and calm.

George got her boat, and then went to fetch

Timmy. The boys hauled the boat down to the sea and they set off to the island. It was easy to row now, because the sea was so calm. They rowed around to the far side of the island, and there was the wreck, piled high on some sharp rocks. It looked a sad and forlorn old ship – but to the four children it was the most exciting thing in the whole world.

Go to **74**.

70

If you have arrived from **81**, *score* ⌀ ⌀ ⌀.

The children watched the old wreck for a little time longer and then went all around the island again. George felt very happy. She had always vowed that she never, never would take anyone there, because it would spoil her island for her. But it hadn't been spoilt. It had made it much nicer.

'We'll wait until the waves go down a bit, then we'll go back home,' she said.

They said very little as they rowed home. They were all tired after the excitements of the day.

'Well – here we are back at the beach again, and I'm jolly glad,' said Julian. 'I'm so hungry I could eat a larder full of things.'

It wasn't long before they were all sitting down to a good tea.

Go to **83**.

'Whatever do you suppose Mother would say if we went just after tea?' said George. 'We've got to behave exactly the same way as usual, or Mother will know we are up to something.'

'What shall we do, then?' asked Anne.

Julian turned a table upside down with a crash.

'We'll play wrecks,' he said. 'This is the wreck. Now we're going to explore it.'

The door flew open and an angry, frowning face looked in. It was George's father!

Go to **76**.

'She's stuck there,' said Julian. 'She won't move now.'

'I do hope there was nobody on board,' said Anne.

The sun shone briefly on the wreck, lighting it up. George looked at the others, a bright gleam of excitement in her eyes.

'It's my wreck!' she cried in an excited voice. 'The storm has lifted the ship off the bottom of the sea and lodged it on those rocks!'

'George! We'll be able to row out and get into the wreck now!' shouted Julian. 'We'll be able to explore it from end to end. We may find the bars of gold. Oh, *George*!'

'Let's row out there now!' begged Dick.

If you think they should, go to **77**. *If not, go to* **65**.

73

They went back to the little cove where they had left the boat, and pushed it out. Even in the shelter of the cove the water was rough, and as soon as they got further out the boat began to pitch up and down violently. Poor Anne was very frightened, and she soon began to feel sick. She wished she hadn't drunk so much ginger ale at lunchtime!

George was finding it more and more difficult to row in the strong sea, but she was so excited about seeing her wreck that she struggled on.

'Do you want me to take one of the oars?' asked Julian.

George shook her head. 'I can manage on my own,' she said stubbornly.

Just then, however, an extra-large wave came along, and one of the oars was swept right out of George's hand.

Go to **78**.

74

They tied up the boat to the wreck and clambered aboard. The deck was slippery with seaweed, and the smell was very strong indeed.

'Well, this was the deck,' said George, 'and that's where the men got up and down.' She pointed to a large hole. The remains of an iron ladder were still there. George looked at it.

'It seems to be fairly strong,' she said, 'but I think just one person should go down to start with. If the ladder breaks, we don't all want to be stuck down there.'

Anne peered down into the blackness. She wasn't sure she wanted to go down the ladder at all.

'I'll go!' offered Dick.

'It *is* George's wreck,' said Anne, 'so perhaps *she'd* like to go.'

Julian inspected the ladder. 'It looks quite safe to me,' he said.

If you think Dick should go down the ladder, go to **80**. *If you think George should go down the ladder, go to* **85**. *If you think they should all go down the ladder, go to* **86**.

75

In the ordinary way none of the children liked going to bed early – but with such an exciting thing to look forward to, early to bed seemed different that night.

'It will make the time go quickly,' said Anne. 'Shall we go now?'

'Mother would think we were ill if we went just after tea,' said George. 'No, let's go after supper. We'll just say we're tired with rowing.'

So by eight o'clock all the children were in bed, rather to Aunt Fanny's surprise. George lay awake for some time thinking of her island, her wreck – and, of course, her beloved dog!

Julian woke first in the morning. He sat up in bed and whispered as loudly as he could: 'Dick! Dick! Wake up! We're going to see the wreck!'

Go to **69**.

76

'What was that noise?' asked Uncle Quentin. 'George! Did you overturn that table?'

'I did,' said Julian. 'I'm sorry, Uncle Quentin. I quite forgot you were working.'

'Any more noise like that and I shall keep you all in bed tomorrow!' said his uncle. 'Georgina, keep your cousins quiet!'

'We'd better do something really quiet,' said George as her father closed the door, 'or he'll keep his word – and we'll find ourselves in bed tomorrow just when we want to explore the wreck.'

Go to **62**.

77

'We couldn't possibly risk it now,' said George. 'The waves are much too big and the wind is still very strong.'

'Oh George, please!' said Dick. 'You row so well I'm sure you'll be able to get us there even if the waves are big. And if we leave it for another day somebody else may see the wreck and come and explore it before we've had the chance!'

George thought hard. She knew that the sea was really too rough, but she couldn't bear the idea of someone else exploring her precious wreck before she did.

'All right, we'll go,' she said. 'But you'll have a rough time getting there!'

Go to **73**.

Anne gave a shriek and began to cry.

'We'll all be drowned,' she sobbed. 'Oh Julian, please do something! We'll never get back to shore now. Oh help!'

'Be quiet, you silly baby,' said George, who was very frightened herself but refused to show it.

'Don't talk to Anne like that,' said Dick. 'She can't help being frightened.'

'And you can keep quiet too,' said George furiously. 'You're the one who wanted to explore the wreck straight away instead of waiting until the weather was better.'

All this time the boat was tossing up and down on the rough sea. George tried her best to steer it with the oar that was left, but it was no good.

Go to **81**.

When Julian woke the next morning the sun was shining brilliantly. He looked at his watch and was horrified to see that it was half-past seven!

'Dick! Dick! Wake up!' he whispered as loudly as he could. 'We've overslept, and if we don't get out of the house soon Aunt Fanny and Uncle Quentin will be awake and they'll want to know what we're up to!'

He rushed next door and woke George and Anne.

'Come on!' he said, shaking George. 'We've overslept. We must get dressed and go out as quickly as possible.'

Anne and George jumped out of bed and began to dress.

Go to **69**.

80

'Dick can go,' George said generously, 'but he'll need a torch.'

'Here, borrow mine,' offered Julian.

'Do be careful, Dick!' said Anne.

Dick, thrilled to be sent exploring on his own, swung himself carefully on to the top of the iron ladder, and climbed slowly down. A moment or two later he called up to them.

'I'm in a sort of cabin, I think. Goodness, it's dark!'

Go to **90**.

81

Anne cried harder and harder, and Dick had gone quite white. Julian was scared too, and he had no idea what to do. Timmy was barking frantically. Suddenly George gave a cry.

'Quick, Julian, quick! There's the other oar! Look, over there. Grab hold of it, one of you!'

Julian leant over the side of the little boat and just managed to catch the oar as it floated past. He gave it to George, who began to row back towards the island. It was much easier going back because the waves helped to carry them along. Soon they were back in the little cove, and thankfully pulled the boat up on to the sand.

'It's no good,' said George. 'We must wait until tomorrow. It'll be a good idea to come early. I expect lots of grown-ups will think it's their business to explore it too.'

Go to **70**.

82

'It *is* an old cup!' said Anne, picking it up. 'And here's half a saucer. Perhaps the captain was having a cup of tea when the ship went down.'

This made the children feel rather odd. George gave a shiver. 'Let's go,' she said. 'I don't like it much. It *is* exciting, I know, but it's a bit frightening too!'

As they turned to go, Julian flashed the torch around the cabin for the last time. He was about to switch it off and follow the others when he caught sight of something that made him stop. He shone his torch on it, then called to the others: 'I say! Wait a bit! There's a cupboard here in the wall.

Let's see if there's anything in it!' He tried to prise it open with his fingers.

'I wonder if it's locked?' said Anne.

If you think the cupboard is locked, go to **91**. *If not, go to* **84**.

83

'Did you have an exciting day?' asked their aunt.

'Oh yes,' said Anne eagerly. 'The storm was grand. The sea threw up . . .'

Julian and Dick both kicked her under the table. Anne stared at the boys angrily, tears in her eyes.

'Now what's the matter?' asked Aunt Fanny. 'Did somebody kick you, Anne? Well, really, this kicking under the table has got to stop. What did the sea throw up, dear?'

'It threw up the most enormous waves,' said Anne, looking defiantly at the others. 'But I wasn't really afraid of the storm. In fact, I wasn't nearly as afraid of it as Ti . . .'

Everyone interrupted her at once, speaking very loudly.

'The rabbits were so tame.'

'We watched some jackdaws,' said Julian and Dick together.

Aunt Fanny laughed. 'You sound like a lot of jackdaws yourselves,' she said. 'Now, have you all finished? Then you had better go and play quietly in the other room. But don't disturb your father, George. He's very busy.'

'We'll have to be up most awfully early,' said Dick a little later. 'I'm tired with all that rowing. What about going to bed in good time tonight?'

If you think they should go to bed early, go to **75**. *If not, go to* **71**.

84

If you have arrived from **88**, *score* ⌒.

There was a wooden handle on the door. George tugged at it. The door, rotten with seawater, fell off in her hand! They all crowded around the cupboard. Julian flashed his torch over the inside.

'It's empty,' said Anne in disappointment. 'I thought there was going to be something splendid inside!'

'Never mind,' said Julian. 'Let's go and explore the rest of the ship.' As Julian turned to go out of the cabin his torch lit up a dark corner.

'Wait a minute!' he shouted. 'Look, there's another cupboard in this corner! Let's see if there's anything in it.'

Go to **96**.

85

'I'll go,' said George firmly. 'I've always wanted to know what this wreck was like, and I'm going to be the first to explore it.'

The others agreed that this was fair, so George made her way to the ladder and climbed carefully down. It was dark and smelly in the space below the deck, and George began to feel that the wreck was really more pleasant sunk under the water than raised above it!

She felt her way along, holding her torch in front of her. It was very slippery underfoot because of all the seaweed. It gave her a funny feeling to be inside the wreck she had thought about for so long.

Go to **87**.

86

If you have arrived from **67**, *score* ◁ ◁ ◁.

'All right,' said George. 'I've got a torch. Follow me!' She swung herself down the ladder and the others followed. The light from the torch showed a very strange sight. The floor was almost entirely covered with seaweed, and the children had to bend their heads in places because the ceilings were so low. The smell of drying seaweed was horrible! Around them were several doors leading to little cabins.

Soon they came to a bigger cabin than the others they had seen. It had a bunk in one corner, in which a large crab rested. Wooden shelves, festooned with grey-green seaweed, hung crookedly on the walls.

'This must have been the captain's own cabin,'

said Julian. 'It's the biggest one. Look, what's that in the corner? It looks like some sort of cup!'

If you think it is a cup, go to **82**. *If not, go to* **94**.

87

Gradually she worked her way across the space, flashing the torch around the walls to see if there was a chest or cupboard that might contain gold bars. She didn't see anything, though, and eventually she came to a gap in the wall that had once been a door. She climbed carefully over a beam that had fallen across the doorway and shone the torch around the walls. She could see that she was in a small cabin, with the remains of a bunk and a table in it.

Go to **93**.

88

Julian took it from George. 'Let me have a look,' he said.

He stared at the thing for a minute or two. It looked exactly like a hollow ball that had been cut cleanly in half.

'Golly!' said Dick. 'I think I know what it is! It's half of a globe! The captain must have had a globe for navigation in his cabin, and it must have fallen apart when the ship was wrecked.'

'I think you're right,' said Julian. He put the half-globe back on the floor, while George examined the cabin walls.

'Gosh, look, there's a cupboard,' she said. 'I wonder if it's locked?'

If you think the cupboard is locked, go to **91**. *If not, go to* **84**.

89

The children looked at the box. It had burst open and showed a tin lining that was waterproof. Whatever was in the box would not be spoilt – it would be quite dry!

Dick ran to pick it up.

'I said, what's this on the ground?' shouted his uncle.

'It's . . . something that belongs to us,' said Dick, going red.

'Well, I shall take it away from you,' said his uncle. 'Disturbing me like this! Give it to me. Where did you get it?'

He glared at poor Anne, who was nearest.

'Out of the wreck,' stammered the girl, scared.

'Out of the *wreck*!' said her uncle in surprise. 'The old wreck that was thrown up yesterday? I heard about that. Do you mean to say you've been in it?'

'Yes,' said Dick.

'Well, this box may contain something important,' said Uncle Quentin, and he took the box from

Dick's hands. 'You've no right to go prying about in that old wreck.'

'Well, it's *my* wreck,' muttered George.

But her father, taking no notice of George, turned and went into the house, carrying the box.

Go to **108**.

90

It was very cold and gloomy and smelly inside the ship. Dick had to bend his head to get about, the ceilings were so low. His feet slipped on the seaweed, too. As he shone the torch around he could see part of a trapdoor.

'I expect that's where they stored the cargo,' he said to himself. 'I wonder what kind of things the ship used to carry?'

Suddenly he spied what looked like the door of a cabin. Feeling very excited, he started to move towards it, missed his footing on the slippery seaweed and fell over! The torch hit the deck and went out.

Go to **67**.

91

If you have arrived from **88**, *score* ⌒⌐.

Julian tried to prise open the door with his fingers, but it wouldn't move. 'It's locked,' he said. 'Of course, it would be!'

'I expect the lock is rotten by now,' said George, and she tried too. Then she took out her big strong pocket-knife and inserted it between the cupboard door and the cabin wall. She forced back the blade – and the lock of the cupboard suddenly snapped! The door swung open, and the children saw a shelf inside with a few curious objects on it.

There was a wooden box, swollen with the wet. There were a few things that looked like old, pulpy books, and two or three objects so spoiled by sea water that no one could possibly say what they were.

'Nothing very interesting – except the box,' said Julian, and he picked it up. On the top were stamped initials – H.J.K.

'I expect those were the captain's initials,' said Dick.

'No, they were the initials of my great-great-great-grandfather, Henry John Kirrin!' said George, her eyes shining. 'This must have been his very private box in which he kept old papers or diaries. We simply *must* open it!'

Go to **100**.

92

'The box will be quite safe under my bed until tomorrow,' said George. 'Then we can try to open it.'

They smuggled the box up the stairs and into

George's room without Uncle Quentin or Aunt Fanny seeing them.

'What are you all planning to do tomorrow?' asked Aunt Fanny at teatime.

'Er . . . we're not quite sure,' said Julian, before anyone else could say anything. They all knew that the first thing they were going to do the next day was to try to open the mysterious box!

All of them had trouble getting to sleep that night, they were so excited about what they might find in the box.

Go to **102**.

93

Perhaps this was the captain's cabin, thought George.

There was no sign of a chest, though, and she was just about to make her way out again when she suddenly spied a cupboard in one corner. In great excitement she tried to open it, but the door was locked. She took out the big strong pocket-knife that she always carried and inserted it between the cupboard and the cabin wall. The lock, which was rotten, snapped, and the door swung open!

Go to **98**.

94

'No, it's much too big for a cup,' said Anne, picking it up. 'It feels very heavy. I think it's made of metal, but it's hard to tell with all this seaweed on it.'

'Let me have a look at it,' said George, who really felt that she should be the first one to make *any* discovery on her precious wreck. 'Here, somebody hold my torch.'

George turned the strange object over in her hands.

'There are some lines on it,' she said. 'Rather wavy lines – almost like a drawing of something.'

Go to **88**.

95

If you have arrived from **110**, *score* ◠◠.

Julian found a chisel in the shed and tried to force the lid of the box, but the chisel slipped and jabbed his fingers. Then he tried other things, but the box obstinately refused to open.

'I know what to do,' said Anne. 'Let's take it to the top of the house and throw it down to the ground. It would burst open then, I expect.'

'Well, it might be worth trying,' said Julian.

He carried the box up to the attic and opened the window. Then he hurled the box out of the window as violently as he could. It flew through the air and landed with a crash on the crazy paving.

At once the french windows opened and Uncle Quentin came out like a bullet from a gun. 'Whatever are you doing?' he cried. 'Surely you aren't

throwing things at each other out of the window. What's this on the ground?'

Go to **89**.

96

But the cupboard was locked. George got out her pocket-knife and managed to prise the door open. Inside were a few old glasses, a book, pulpy with water, and a wooden box. Julian lifted out the box.

'Look!' he said. 'There are some initials on it – H.J.K.'

'Those are my great-great-great-grandfather's

initials,' said George. 'This box must have belonged to him. We simply *must* open it!'

Go to **100**.

97

They took it in turns to watch Uncle Quentin's study, but most annoyingly he remained in it all morning. Aunt Fanny was surprised to see one or two of the children always about the garden that day, instead of down on the beach.

'Doesn't your father *ever* go out?' said Dick to George when it was their turn to keep watch.

'Well, not very often,' said George. 'But I'll tell you what – he may go to sleep this afternoon. He sometimes does that.'

Julian was left behind in the garden that afternoon. He sat down under a tree and opened a book. Soon he heard a curious noise that made him look up.

'That's Uncle Quentin snoring!' he said to himself in excitement. 'I wonder if I could possibly creep in at the french windows and get our box!'

He stole into the study. The box was on a table beside his uncle's chair. Standing behind the chair, Julian reached out and very carefully began to lift the box.

And then a bit of the broken wood of the box fell to the floor with a thud!

Does this wake Uncle Quentin? If it does, go to **105**. *If it doesn't, go to* **115**.

98

Inside were a few old books, pulpy with water, some sort of glass drinking-vessel, cracked in half, and a wooden box.

'Well, there certainly aren't any gold bars in *here*,' George said to herself. 'That old box is the only thing that looks at all interesting. I'll take it back up on deck to show the others. I wonder if I can get it open?'

But she couldn't prise it open with her pocket-knife, so she took it back to where the others waited on deck.

'Oh look,' said Dick. 'It's got the captain's initials on it – H.J.K.'

'No, they were the initials of my great-great-great-grandfather,' said George. 'His name was Henry John Kirrin. This must have been the very private box he kept his papers in. We simply *must* open it!'

Go to **100**.

99

George was trembling all over with excitement.

'If only we could find it!' she whispered. 'If only we could!'

'We'll have a jolly good hunt for it,' said Julian. 'It will be awfully difficult because the castle is in ruins now, and so overgrown. But somehow or other we'll find those ingots!' Then he frowned. 'What are we going to do about the box? I mean, George's father will notice that it isn't there. We'll have to give it back.'

'Well, can't we take the map out and keep it?' said Dick. 'We're pretty certain he hasn't looked in the box, so he won't miss it. No – I've got a better idea! Let's take a copy of the map. Then we can put the real one back and replace the box.'

They all voted that a very good idea. They went back to Kirrin Cottage and traced the map carefully. They did it in the toolshed because they didn't want anyone to see them. It was an odd map. It was in three parts.

Go to **113**.

100

If you have arrived from **96** *or* **98**, *score* ⌒⌐.

It was quite impossible to force the lid with the tools they had with them.

'We'll open it at home,' said Julian, his voice sounding rather excited. 'We'll get a hammer or something. Oh George – this really is a find!'

They all went back to where they had tied up George's boat, clambered in and started to row home. As they rowed they saw that others beside themselves had found out that the wreck had been thrown up from the bottom of the sea.

'Golly! Half the boats in the bay have discovered it!' cried Julian, looking around at the fishing-smacks that had come as near to the wreck as they dared. When they saw the children on board they yelled hello loudly.

'Ahoy there! What's that ship?'

'It's the old wreck!' Julian yelled back. 'She was thrown up yesterday in the storm!'

'Don't say any more,' said George, frowning. 'It's *my* wreck. I don't want sightseers on it!'

No more was said, and the four children rowed home as fast as they could. On the way back they discussed the best place to hide the box.

'Under my bed,' suggested George.

'No, Aunt Fanny might find it there,' said Julian. 'She doesn't come into our room much. Shall I hide it under my bed?'

*If you think they should hide the box under George's bed, go to **92**. If you think they should hide it under Julian's bed, go to **103**.*

101

Julian took a few steps backwards and waited behind Uncle Quentin's chair. After what seemed like hours, his uncle lifted his hand from the box, scratched his head and let his hand fall back on to the arm of the chair.

Julian hardly dared to breath! He crept forward, and was about to pick up the box when he heard Aunt Fanny walk past the study door, singing to herself.

Go to **105**.

102

They were all up bright and early the following morning, and were pleased to see it was another fine day. Aunt Fanny was in rather a hurry to get breakfast over.

'What are you in such a rush for, Mother?' asked George.

'I've got a lot to do today,' said her mother. 'I'm going to give your room a good turning out, George. It really is frightfully untidy.'

The children looked at each other in horror, thinking of the precious box hidden under George's bed.

Suddenly Dick had an idea. '*A-ti-shoo!*' he went.

'Goodness, Dick! I do hope you're not getting a cold,' said his aunt.

'Well, I think I'd better go up and get a handkerchief,' said Dick.

He raced upstairs, and was just about to dash into George's room when Uncle Quentin came out of the bathroom.

'What are you up to, Dick?' he asked. 'Why are you going into George's room?'

'I came up to get a handkerchief,' said Dick, 'and . . . er . . . I suddenly remembered that I hadn't got any clean ones, so I thought I'd see if Anne had.'

'Well, hurry up and get one,' said his uncle. 'You children ought to be out and about on a day like this.' He showed no sign of going downstairs, so poor Dick hastily had to find a handkerchief in one of Anne's drawers, and, under his uncle's watchful eye, return to the others.

Go to **110**.

103

They decided to hide the box under Julian's bed.

'We'll open it tomorrow morning,' he said. 'I can't wait!'

After breakfast the next day they took the precious box out to the toolshed. They were simply longing to force it open. All of them secretly felt certain that it would hold treasure of some sort.

Go to **95**.

104

The following morning the newspapers were full of the extraordinary way in which the old wreck had been thrown up out of the sea. The newspaper men had got out of the children's uncle the tale of the wreck and the lost gold, and some of them had even managed to land on Kirrin Island and take pictures of the old ruined castle. Now sightseers from all around were coming to the island.

George was furious.

'It's *my* castle!' she stormed at her mother. 'It's *my* island! You said it could be mine. You did, you did!'

'I know, George dear,' said her mother. 'But you really must be sensible. It can't hurt the island to be landed on, and it can't hurt the castle or the wreck to be photographed.'

'But I don't want them to be,' said George, her face sulky.

All morning she hung about the garden, looking crossly out towards the sea. Julian tried to comfort her.

'Listen! No one knows our secret. We'll wait for this excitement to die down and then we'll go to Kirrin Castle and find the ingots!'

But then something dreadful happened!

Go to **112**.

105

If you have arrived from **101**, *score* ◁ ◁.

His uncle moved in his chair and opened his eyes.

'What's that?' Julian heard his uncle say. Julian didn't move. Then his uncle settled down again and shut his eyes. Soon there was the sound of his rhythmic snoring.

'Hurrah!' thought Julian. 'He's off again!'

He picked up the box, slipped out of the french windows and ran to the beach, where the others were lying in the sun.

'Hi!' he yelled, dropping down on the sand with a grin. 'Hi! I've got it! Now – let's see what's in here. I don't believe your father's even tried to look!'

He hadn't. The tin lining was intact. It had rusted with the years of lying in the wet, and the lid was so tightly fitted down that it was almost impossible to move it.

But once George began to work at it with her pocket-knife, scraping away the rust, it began to loosen – and in about a quarter of an hour it came off!

Go to **111**.

106

'It's a map of Kirrin Island!' said George. 'Look, you can see that the castle is marked on it, and the little cove where we left the boat!'

'Gosh! Maybe there'll be some clue about where the gold might be!' exclaimed Anne loudly.

'Ssh!' said George, scowling at her. 'We don't want everyone on the beach to know about the treasure. There are enough people poking about *my* island now that the wreck's been thrown up.'

Anne hung her head. She never could remember to guard her tongue!

They all studied the map very closely, but none of them could really make out what was on it. There were odd squiggles in various places, and the castle was very clearly marked, but they couldn't identify anything else.

'If only we could see properly,' said Dick. 'What we need is a magnifying glass.'

Go to **114**.

107

'What are you doing, Julian?' asked Uncle Quentin.

Julian turned around, shaking from head to foot. Obviously the others hadn't been able to keep Uncle Quentin in the kitchen!

'Oh . . . er . . . I was . . . er,' he stammered.

'I suppose you were trying to take that box away,' said his uncle. 'I told you this morning, I'm going to look after that box in case it contains something important. Now put it down, and don't let me catch you in my study again!'

Julian could hardly believe it! His uncle thought that he was taking the box, not bringing it back. And it was obvious he hadn't even noticed it had been gone for a while. Mumbling, 'Sorry, Uncle Quentin,' he hurried off to find the others. Just then he heard the telephone ring, and Aunt Fanny went to answer it. She soon came back.

Who is the call for? If you think it's for Julian, go to **124**.
If you think it's for Uncle Quentin, go to **118**.

108

They all thought it was very unfair of Uncle Quentin to take the box.

'Listen,' said Julian. 'We'll get that box back somehow. I'm sure your father won't bother himself with it, George. He'll start writing his book again and forget all about it. I'll wait my chance and slip into his study and get it.'

Go to **97**.

109

Julian waited outside the kitchen until George signalled that the coast was clear.

'My father's just gone into the dining-room for tea,' she whispered. 'I don't think he's missed the box at all!'

Julian slipped through into the study and replaced the box on the table.

He winked at the others when he came back. They felt relieved. They were all scared of Uncle Quentin and weren't at all anxious to be in his bad books. Anne was so terribly afraid she might give something away that she didn't say one word during the whole of the meal.

While they were at tea the telephone rang and Aunt Fanny went to answer it. She soon came back.

Who is the call for? If you think it's for Uncle Quentin, go to **118**. *If you think it's for Julian, go to* **124**.

110

One look at Dick's face as he came into the room told the others that he had not been able to move the box from under George's bed.

The children were all very quiet during the rest of the meal, as they racked their brains to think of a way to move the box before Aunt Fanny found it.

'Well,' said their aunt, 'if you've finished you can all get down. Why don't you go out into the garden?'

Julian suddenly had a brainwave.

'I've just remembered that I haven't cleaned my teeth this morning. I'll nip upstairs and do it.'

This time the coast was clear, and, grabbing the box from under George's bed, Julian was about to hide it in his own room when he realised that the best thing to do would be to take it down to the toolshed so that they could all try to open it. He could hardly wait to see what was in it!

Go to **95**.

The children bent over the box eagerly. Inside lay some old papers and a book of some kind with a black cover. Nothing else at all. No bar of gold. No treasure. Everyone felt a little disappointed.

'It's all quite dry,' said Julian, surprised. 'The tin lining kept everything perfect.'

He picked up the book and opened it.

'It's a diary your great-great-great-grandfather kept of the ship's voyages,' he said. 'I can hardly read the writing, it's so small and funny.'

George picked up one of the papers. It was made of thick parchment, quite yellow with age. She spread it out on the sand and looked at it.

It seemed to be a kind of map.

'Perhaps it's a map of some place he had to go to,' suggested Julian. But suddenly George's hands began to shake, and her eyes gleamed brilliantly as she looked at the others. She opened her mouth but didn't speak.

'What's the matter?' said Julian curiously. 'Have you lost your tongue?'

George began to speak with a rush. 'Do you know what this map is of?'

'Kirrin Island!' and 'Kirrin Castle!' guessed Dick and Anne, both together.

If you think George is looking at a map of Kirrin Island, go to **106**. *If you think she is looking at a map of Kirrin Castle, go to* **119**.

112

Uncle Quentin sold the box to a man who bought antiques! He came out from his study, beaming, and told Aunt Fanny and the children.

'You know that old tin-lined box from the wreck?' he said to his wife. 'Well, this fellow collects curious things like that, and he gave me a very good price for it. As soon as he saw the old map there and the old diary he said he would buy the whole collection.'

The children stared at him in horror. Now someone else would study that map and perhaps jump to what 'ingots' meant! Nobody could fail to know what the map showed if they studied it carefully. When they were alone the children discussed the whole matter.

'Now listen!' said Julian at last. 'We'll ask Aunt Fanny if we can go to Kirrin Island and spend a day or two there – sleep there at night, I mean. That will give us a little time to poke around and see what we can find.'

When they went to ask Aunt Fanny, Uncle Quentin was with her. He was all smiles.

'Well,' he said. 'What's this deputation for?'

'We just wanted to ask if we might go for the weekend to Kirrin Castle, and spend a day or two on the island. You can't think how much we'd love to!'

'Please say yes,' pleaded George.

If you think Uncle Quentin will say yes, go to **123**. *If you think he will say no, go to* **116**.

113

'This part shows the dungeons under the castle,' said Julian. 'And this shows a plan of the ground floor of the castle – and this shows the top part. My word, it was a fine place in those days! The dungeons run all under the castle. I wonder how people got down to them.'

'We'll have to study the map a bit more and see,' said George. 'It all looks rather muddled to us at present – but once we take the map over to the castle and study it there we may be able to make out how to get down to the hidden dungeons. I say – there can't be many children who have ever had such an adventure as this!'

Julian put the traced map carefully in his jeans pocket. Then he placed the real map back into the box and looked towards the house.

'What about putting the box back now?' he asked. 'Maybe your father is still asleep, George.'

But he wasn't. He was awake. As the children walked up the front path they could hear him talking to Aunt Fanny in the kitchen.

To get to the study, Julian either had to go through the kitchen or try the french windows again.

If you think he should risk the kitchen, go to **109**. *If you think he should try the french windows, go to* **120**.

114

'Of course!' said George, jumping up. 'I think there's one in Father's study. I'll tell him we've found something interesting on the beach and we want to get a closer look at it. With any luck he'll think it's a shell or something.' And she ran off along the beach.

Ten minutes later she came back with the magnifying glass.

'Father's still asleep,' she said, 'so I just took the glass. I'll put it back before he knows we've borrowed it.'

But though they examined every inch of the map, there was nothing on it at all that gave any clue to where the treasure might be found.

'Oh well,' said George gloomily. 'I suppose it was too good to be true to think that we might find the treasure.'

She picked up the map to put it back in the box, but it slipped through her fingers and fell on to the sand, wrong side up. George picked it up. There seemed to be something on the back. She had a quick look, then looked again more carefully. She gave a shout.

'Look! Look! There's another map on the back!'

'A map of what?' asked Julian.

Go to **119**.

115

Uncle Quentin stirred in his sleep and grunted. He shifted in his chair, flinging out his hand. To his horror, Julian saw the hand come to rest right on top of the box! There was no way he could pick up the box now without waking his uncle.

Go to **101**.

116

Uncle Quentin looked thoughtful.

'Spend the weekend on the island! What a very

strange idea,' he said. 'There's nowhere for you to sleep, for a start, and what would you eat?'

'We could sleep in the castle,' said George. 'One of the rooms has still got a roof, and Mother will give us plenty of food to take with us. Oh please, Father, do say we can!'

'I must think it over,' said her father. 'I'll let you know what I've decided later today.'

'Oh Father!' yelled George. 'You are mean! Why won't you tell us now? I think you're horrible to keep us waiting!'

Julian tried to kick George to make her stop, but it was too late.

'That settles it,' said Uncle Quentin. 'You're not going.' And he left the room.

Go to **127**.

117

Julian stared at his uncle. He knew that grown-ups could do exactly as they liked, and that if his uncle wanted to sell the castle and the island, he could. But his uncle didn't know about the gold ingots! Julian wondered whether to tell him. Then he thought that perhaps he should talk to the others about it first.

'When are you going to sell the island, Uncle?' he asked quietly.

'The deeds will be signed in about a week's

time,' was the answer. 'So if you really want to spend a day or two there, you'd better do it quickly.'

'Was it the man who bought the old box who wants to buy the island?' asked Julian.

'Yes, it was,' replied his uncle.

The children went out into the garden to discuss the dreadful news.

'Shall we tell Uncle Quentin what we think is hidden in the castle?' said Dick.

If you think they should tell Uncle Quentin, go to **121**. *If not, go to* **129**.

118

If you have arrived from **107** *or* **124**, *score* ⌒ɔ.

'It's for you, Quentin,' said Aunt Fanny, standing in the doorway. 'Apparently the old wreck has caused quite a lot of excitement, and there are men from a London newspaper who want to ask you questions about it.'

'Tell them I'll see them at six,' said Uncle Quentin.

The children looked at one another in alarm. They hoped that their uncle wouldn't show the box to the newspaper men. If he did, then the secret of the hidden gold might come out!

'What a mercy we took a tracing of the map!' said Julian after tea. 'But I'm sorry now we left the real map in the box. Someone else may guess our secret!'

Go to **104**.

119

If you have arrived from **114**, *score* ⌢ ⌢.

'It's Kirrin Castle!' shouted George. 'It's a map of my old castle, when it wasn't a ruin. And it shows the dungeons! And look – just look what's written in this corner of the dungeons!'

She put a trembling finger on one part of the map. The others leaned over to see what it was – and printed in old-fashioned letters was a curious word: INGOTS.

'Ingots!' said Anne, puzzled. 'What does that mean? I've never heard that word before.'

But the two boys had. 'Ingots!' cried Dick. 'Why – that must be the bars of gold. They were called ingots.'

'Most bars of metal are called ingots,' said Julian, going red with excitement. 'But as we know there is gold missing from that ship, then it really looks as if ingots here meant bars of gold. Oh, George! To think the gold may still be hidden somewhere under Kirrin Castle!'

Go to **99**.

'Golly,' said George. 'What shall we do now? We must get the box into the study again, but if Father sees us with it he'll be very angry.'

They looked at each other in dismay.

'Well,' said Julian, 'I'll just have to try to sneak into the study while he isn't looking. I'll tell you what – you three go into the kitchen and try to keep Uncle Quentin talking while I go into the study by the french windows.'

'But what are we going to talk to him about?' asked Anne nervously. She found it very difficult to talk to her fierce uncle at any time.

'Oh we'll ask him about the tides or something,' said George. 'He knows a lot about that sort of thing.'

While the others went into the kitchen, Julian waited a few moments, then slipped through the french windows. He was just about to put the box down on the table when a voice behind him made him jump!

Go to **107**.

Go to **107**.

121

'He won't believe us,' said Anne in despair. 'He'll think we're only doing it to try to stop him selling the island.'

'It might be worth a try,' said Julian. 'After all, he knows the story of the lost gold.'

'I bet he jolly well doesn't believe you,' said George sulkily. 'I think he's an absolute beast to sell my island.'

'Well,' said Dick. 'Let's try it and see what happens. Come on.'

They all went back to the study to find Uncle Quentin, who was reading one of his scientific books.

'Uncle Quentin,' said Julian, 'we've got something to tell you.'

Go to **133**.

122

At that moment one of the old, rusted iron rungs snapped!

George gave a shriek as her feet slipped off the ladder. She tried to hang on, but she couldn't quite manage it, and she fell in an awkward heap on to the projecting slab. Timmy gave a surprised '*Woof*!' when his beloved mistress fell down on top of him!

The other children were all peering anxiously down the well.

'George! George! Are you all right?' shouted Dick.

George sat up very carefully on the slab. She was afraid that any sudden movement might shake the slab loose and send her and Timmy to the bottom of the well. Her knees were sore, so were her elbows, and she could feel a trickle of blood running down her face from where she had scratched it on the ladder, but apart from that she seemed to be in one piece.

'Yes, I'm fine!' she shouted back. 'But how are Timmy and I going to get out of here?'

Go to **145**.

123

If you have arrived from **130**, *score* ◁ ◁ ◁.

'If you want to, you can,' said Uncle Quentin. 'You won't have a chance to soon. My dears, we have had a marvellous offer for Kirrin Island! A man wants to buy it, rebuild the castle as a hotel, and make it into a proper holiday place. What do you think of that!'

All four children stared at the smiling man, shocked and horrified. Somebody was going to buy the island! Had their secret been discovered? Did the man want to buy the castle because he had read the map, and knew there was plenty of gold hidden there?

George gave a curious choke. Her eyes burned as if they were on fire.

'Mother! You can't sell my island! You can't sell my castle. I won't let them be sold!'

She turned and stumbled out of the room.

Go to **117**.

If you have arrived from **107**, *score* ⌒⌐.

'Julian,' said Aunt Fanny, 'it's your mother on the telephone.'

Julian picked up the receiver.

'Hello, Mother,' he said. 'Are you and Father having a good time?'

'Yes, thank you,' replied his mother. 'How are all of you? I do hope you're enjoying yourselves. What have you been doing?'

'Oh, we've been swimming, and we've been for walks, and George has taken us out in the boat. We're having a super time!' Julian replied.

'Is George one of the local children you've made friends with?' asked his mother. 'What about your cousin Georgina? Don't you spend any time with her? I'm sure your uncle and aunt want you to keep her company.'

'Oh Mother,' said Julian, laughing, 'George isn't one of the local boys! George is Georgina. She hates being a girl, and won't answer if you call her Georgina.'

'She's a funny girl,' replied his mother. 'Still, I'm glad you are all having a good time. Give my love to the others.'

'I will,' said Julian. 'Goodbye, Mother.'

He put down the receiver and went back to the tea table, but just then the telephone rang again.

'What, again?' said Aunt Fanny, putting down her tea cup. She went out to the kitchen and picked up the receiver. 'Just a moment,' she said into it.

Go to **118**.

125

Anne and Julian went back out into the great yard in the centre of the castle. The stone floor was overgrown with grass and weeds.

'This would be a good place to begin looking,' said Anne. 'Shall I go and get a spade?'

'No, not yet,' said Julian. 'We'll have a really good look around and then see if we can find anything that looks exciting.'

He started to walk around the broken-down walls of the yard, looking for anything that might give a clue as to where the entrance to the dungeons might be. Anne did the same on the other side of the yard.

'No,' said Julian, after he had gone all the way around. 'I can't find a thing!'

Anne thought it would have been much easier if she had had any idea of what she was looking for! She couldn't imagine what the entrance to dungeons might look like, and was secretly rather afraid of having to go into them when they'd been found.

Go to **136**.

*If you have arrived from **137**, score ⌒.*

'No, let's not,' said George. 'We all need to search for the dungeons.'

'Come on,' said Julian. 'You take the spades, Dick, I'll take the food and drink with Anne, and George can take the other things.'

They put everything into the little room and piled the rugs and blankets in the corners. They all thought it would be most exciting to spend the night there.

'Well, now we'll get down to business,' said Julian, pulling the map out of his pocket. 'We must study this really carefully, and find out exactly under what spots the entrances to the dungeons are.'

*Go to **140**.*

George's face went scarlet, and she was trying not to cry. Boys didn't cry. She rushed off into the garden.

Anne went after her. She found George sitting under a tree, looking very sulky.

'Go away!' said George.

'Look,' said Anne. 'Why don't you go and tell your father you're sorry you were rude to him. Perhaps then he'll let us go.'

'No,' said George. 'I'm not sorry, and it would be a lie to say so. My father always spoils everything.'

Anne went sadly back to the house. She was sorry that George was in trouble, and she was even more sorry that they couldn't go and stay on the island.

Go to **130**.

128

But it was just the corner of one of the stone slabs that stuck up even more than the others. Disappointed, Dick went off to get the lemonade.

Julian and Anne were in the little room.

'Did you find anything?' asked Anne eagerly.

'No,' said Dick, 'not yet, though we haven't looked at all the little rooms. I came to get a drink. George and I are both thirsty.'

'I thought we might have lunch,' said Julian. 'Anne and I are starving. Go and get George and we'll eat it now.'

Go to **146**.

129

'No,' said Julian, 'not while there's a chance we can find the gold first. The man who bought the old box has obviously found the map and jumped to the same idea that we did – the store of hidden ingots is somewhere on that island . . . and he's going to get it! Oh dear, this is a horrible thing to happen!'

He put his arm around George, who was obviously very upset, and for once George didn't push it off. Tears came into her eyes, and she angrily tried to blink them away.

Go to **135**.

130

Left alone, George started to calm down. She really wanted to spend the night on her beloved island with her cousins, and so, after thinking things over very carefully, she went back to the house to find her father.

He was in his study. Her mother was there too, and they both looked very pleased about something.

'What is it, George?' asked her mother.

'I wanted to say I was sorry for being rude to Father,' said George.

'Oh, that's all right,' said her father. 'Just don't do it again. Now then – I have some exciting news for you. Fetch your cousins and I'll tell you all about it.'

When Dick, Anne and Julian were all in the study, George asked, 'What is it? May we spend the night on Kirrin Island after all?'

Go to **123**.

If you have arrived from **143**, *score* ◯�.

'Quick! Let's row after it!' George took a firm hold of both oars and swung the boat around. But someone was quicker than she was! Timmy had seen the paper fly from Julian's hand. With an enormous splash he leapt into the water and swam valiantly after the map.

He soon had the map in his mouth and was swimming back to the boat. The children thought he was simply marvellous.

George hauled him into the boat and took the map from his mouth. It was wet, and the children looked anxiously at it to see if the tracing had been spoilt. But it was quite all right.

Go to **141**.

A shower of sand and earth was thrown up as Timmy tried to go down the hole after the rabbit.

'Tim! Do you hear me? Come out of there!' shouted George. 'You're not to chase the rabbits. Come out!'

But Timmy didn't come out. He just went on and on scraping away madly. George went to fetch him. Just as she got up to the gorse bush the scraping stopped. There came a scared yelp – and no more noise was heard. George peered under the prickly bush in atonishment. Timmy had disappeared!

'I say, Julian – Timmy's gone,' said George in a scared voice. 'He surely can't have gone down that rabbit's hole, can he? I mean – he's such a big dog!'

There came the sound of a muffled whine from somewhere below the gorse bush.

'He *is* down the hole!' said Julian. 'However are we going to get him out?'

Go to **148**.

133

'Um,' said Uncle Quentin without looking up.

'We've found an old map in that box you sold, and we think it shows where gold ingots are hidden in the castle,' said Julian.

'Um,' said Uncle Quentin again.

'Well, do you think that it would be a good idea not to sell the island until we've had a good chance to see if there really is gold hidden there?' said Julian.

'Oh, no,' said his uncle absently, 'I'm still going to sell it.' And he went back to his book.

It was obvious that Uncle Quentin hadn't listened to a word that Julian had said. The children trooped despondently out of the study and went back to the garden.

Go to **135**.

They set to work with their spades. It was not really difficult to uncover the hole, which had mostly been blocked by the spreading roots of the gorse bush. A big slab had fallen from part of the tower across the well-hole and partly closed it. The weather and the growing gorse bush had done the rest.

It took all the children together to move the slab. Underneath was a very rotten wooden cover that had given way when Timmy's weight fell on it. The well was very deep and very dark.

Julian shone his torch down. And there was Timmy! Many years before, a big slab had fallen down the well itself and had stuck a little way down across the well-hole – and on this cracked slab sat Timmy, his big eyes staring up in fright.

There was an old iron ladder fastened to the side of the well. George was on it before anyone else could get there! Down she went, not caring if the ladder held or not.

'George! Be careful!' Julian shouted down the well. 'That ladder is old and it may give way!'

If you think the ladder gives way, go to **122**. *If not, go to* **144**.

If you have arrived from **133**, *score* ↶.

'Listen, George!' said Julian. 'We mustn't give up

hope. We'll go to Kirrin Island tomorrow and do our very, very best to get down into the dungeons and find the ingots. Thank goodness we took a tracing of the map.'

George cheered up a little. The thought of going to Kirrin Island for a day or two, and taking Timmy, certainly seemed rather good.

'Let's make a list of all the things we'll need,' said Dick. 'Plenty to eat, for a start.'

'And something to drink,' said George. 'There's no water on the island – though I believe there was a well or something years ago that went right down below the level of the sea and provided fresh water. Anyway, I've never found it.'

'Spades,' said Julian solemnly, and scribbled it down.

'Ropes,' said Dick. 'We may want those, too.'

'And torches,' said George. 'It'll be dark in the dungeons.'

Julian wrote them down.

'And we'll take a few tools, too,' he said. 'They may be useful.'

At the end of half an hour they had quite a long list, and everyone felt pleased and excited. George was beginning to recover from her rage and disappointment. It was impossible to sulk for long when she was with the others.

Go to **138**.

Julian went to get a spade, and began to scrape away the weeds and grass from the stones in the yard. Most of them were cracked and no longer lying flat. A lot of sand had blown in too, and as fast as Julian scraped it off the stones it blew back again! Anne worked away as well, but she was very glad when Julian stopped and put his spade down.

'Golly,' he said. 'I'm starving hungry and very thirsty. I wonder where the others are? Let's go back to the little room and see if they're in there.'

Back in the stone room they were soon joined by Dick and George.

Go to **146**.

'I think we should,' said George. 'After all, it would be awful if we found the gold and then someone took it away from us!'

The trouble was, no one wanted to be a guard! They all wanted to put the supplies in the little stone room and start looking for the entrance to the dungeons as quickly as possible.

Anne thought Julian should be guard because he was the oldest. Julian thought George should be guard because it was her island. George thought Dick should be guard because he always noticed

things, and Dick thought Anne should be guard
because she was the youngest!

'This is silly,' said George.

'Perhaps we shouldn't have a guard at all,'
suggested Julian.

Go to **126**.

138

It was very exciting the next morning, setting off in
the boat with all their things neatly packed at one
end.

'Got the map?' said Dick suddenly.

Julian nodded, and took it out of his pocket –
and the wind at once blew it right out of his hands!
It fell into the sea and bobbed there in the wind,
just out of reach. All four children gave a cry of
utter dismay. Their precious map!

'Whatever shall we do?' wailed Anne.

If you think they should row after it, go to **131**. *If you think
George should try to reach it with one of the oars, go to* **143**.

139

They worked their way carefully through the first
of the little rooms, but found nothing that might be
the entrance to the dungeons. They went on to the
next little room and started to work there.

'Oh, it's so hot,' said George. 'I'd love a drink. What about you, Dick?'

'That's a jolly good idea,' said Dick. 'I'll go and get some lemonade.'

He put down his spade and walked over to the entrance of the room. Suddenly he caught his foot in a clump of grass and stumbled.

'Ouch!' he said, rubbing his toes. 'That hurt. There must be a big stone in that clump of grass, or perhaps . . . goodness! I wonder if there's something metal under there?'

He bent to examine the clump of grass more closely. Maybe he would find a handle of some sort under it!

If you think he finds a handle, go to **147**. *If you think he finds a stone, go to* **128**.

140

They all bent over the traced map.

'Now look,' said Julian, putting his finger on the plan of the dungeons. 'These seem to run all along under the castle, and here – and here – are the marks that seem to represent steps or stairs.'

'Yes,' said George. 'I should think they are. Well, if so, there appear to be two ways of getting down into the dungeons. One lot of steps seems to begin somewhere near this little room, and the other seems to start under the tower there. And what do you suppose this thing is here, Julian?'

She put her finger on a circle that was shown not only in the plan of the dungeons, but also in the plan of the ground floor of the castle.

'I can't imagine what this is,' said Julian, puzzled. 'Oh yes, I know what it might be! You said there was an old well somewhere, do you remember? Well, that may be it, I should think. It would have to be very deep to get fresh water right under the sea – so it probably goes down through the dungeons too. Isn't this thrilling?'

Everyone thought it was. They felt happy and excited and eager to begin their search.

'Well,' said Dick, 'what are we going to start on?'

'How about lunch?' suggested George. 'Or should we explore first?'

If you think they should have their lunch now, go to **146**. *If you think they should explore the castle right away, go to* **149**.

141

George took the oars again, and they set off once more to the island. George made her way through the reefs of rocks with a sure hand. It was marvellous to the others how she could slide the boat in between the dangerous rocks and never get a scratch. She brought them safely to the little inlet, and they pulled the boat high up and began to unload their goods.

'We'll carry all the things to that little stone room,' said Julian. 'They'll all be safe there. I hope nobody comes to the island while we're here, George.'

'I shouldn't think they would,' said George. 'Father said it would be about a week before the deeds are signed, so we've got until then, anyhow.'

'Even so,' said Dick, 'perhaps we should set a guard. What do you think, George?'

Does George agree with Dick? If she does, go to **137**. *If she doesn't, go to* **126**.

142

'There are remains of two or three little rooms on the other side of the yard,' said George. 'Let's go and look there, Dick!'

The little rooms on the other side of the yard were full of weeds and sticks dropped by the jackdaws that lived in the old tower of the castle.

'At least we'll be able to make a good fire with all these sticks,' said George. 'The jackdaws must have been dropping them here for years and years.'

They began to scrape away the sticks and weeds with their spades until the old stones of the floor were clear. They were quite smooth, and fitted together with no space between them. Dick tried sticking his spade between one or two, but it didn't work.

Go to **139**.

'Somebody grab it!' yelled Dick. 'Quick, use an oar or something!'

George pulled one of the oars into the boat and leant over the side, frantically trying to reach the map with the other oar. The boat rocked violently. Anne gave a shriek.

'George! Please don't do that! You'll capsize the boat!'

George ignored her and tried again to reach the map, but it was too far away.

'I'll dive in after it,' said Julian, pulling off his sweater.

George made another wild try for the map, again making the boat rock from side to side. Anne started to cry.

'Oh help, the boat will capsize and we'll all be drowned! I wish I'd stayed at Kirrin Cottage with Aunt Fanny,' she sobbed.

'Shut up, Anne!' said Dick fiercely.

Just then an extra-strong puff of wind blew the map much further away from the boat. Julian was struggling out of his jeans, getting ready to dive in after it, but George had a better idea.

Go to **131**.

144

George reached Timmy safely and somehow she got him on to her shoulder and, holding him there with one hand, climbed slowly up again. The other three hauled her out, and Timmy jumped around her, barking and licking for all he was worth!

'Well, Timmy!' said Dick. 'You shouldn't chase rabbits – but you've certainly done us a good turn, because you've found the well for us! Now we've only got to look around a little to find the dungeon entrance!'

Go to **157**.

145

'We'll have to get a rope,' called Julian. 'Wait there, George, and I'll get one!'

George smiled to herself. She could hardly do anything else but wait!

Julian came back with the rope and lowered it down the well.

'Pull Timmy up first,' George shouted up to the others. 'I'll tie the rope around him, and then you can pull him up.'

It wasn't easy getting the rope around Timmy, but he seemed to know that George was trying to help him get out of this nasty dark place, and he stood quite still. George was afraid that any sudden movement might make the slab slip, so she had to work very carefully. At last she had the rope tied around Timmy, rather like a parcel.

'Ready, Julian!' she shouted.

Go to **153**.

146

If you have arrived from **136**, *score* ⌒⌒⌒. *If you have arrived from* **128**, *score* ⌒⌒⌒⌒. *If you have arrived from* **150**, *score* ⌒⌒⌒⌒⌒ .

All the children were very hungry by now, and they eagerly unpacked their food. After lunch they had another look at the map.

'Look,' said George suddenly, putting her finger on the circle that they all thought must be meant to represent the well. 'The entrance to the dungeons seems to be not very far off the well. If only we could find the well, we could hunt around a bit for the beginning of the dungeon steps. The well is shown on both maps. It seems to be somewhere about the middle of the castle.'

'That's a good idea,' said Julian, and they all went out into the middle of the castle. They stood there looking around in vain for anything that might perhaps have been the opening of an old well. It was all so overgrown, and the stones that had once formed the floor of the courtyard were now cracked and were no longer lying flat.

'Look, there's a rabbit!' cried Dick.

Unfortunately, the sight of the rabbit was too much for Timmy! He gave an excited yelp and rushed full tilt at the surprised creature. It tore off at top speed and disappeared under a gorse bush. Timmy went after it.

Go to **132**.

147

It was a handle! A sort of smooth, heavy metal ring!

'George! George!' shouted Dick. 'Come here quickly!'

They worked frantically with their spades to scrape all the grass and earth away from the stone. They could see the handle quite clearly now. They thought this must be the entrance to the dungeons!

'Go and get the others,' Dick said. 'We must show them what we've found!'

George rushed off to find Julian and Anne.

'Come quickly,' she cried. 'We think we've found the entrance!'

Julian and Anne ran back with George to where Dick was waiting.

They all started to scrape away the sand and earth on the stone. Julian tried to stick his spade around the edge to loosen it, and gradually a gap appeared. It took a long time, but at last there was a small space all around the stone.

'Let's try to pull it up now,' said Dick.

He and Julian took hold of the metal ring and pulled hard. The stone moved slightly.

Go to **150**.

148

'We'll have to dig up the gorse bush to begin with,' said George in a determined voice.

The bush was far too big and prickly to creep underneath, so Julian went to fetch an axe. They had brought a small one with them, and it would do to chop away the prickly branches and trunk of the gorse bush.

By the time the bush had been reduced to a mere stump, they could see the hole quite well. Julian shone his torch down it. He gave a shout of surprise.

'I know what's happened! The old well is here. The rabbits had a hole at the side of it – and Timmy scraped away to make it bigger. He uncovered a bit of the well-hole – and he's fallen down the well!'

'Oh no, oh no,' cried George in panic. 'Oh Timmy, are you all right?'

A distant whine came to their ears. Evidently Tim was there somewhere. The children looked at one another.

'We must get our spades and dig out the hole of the well,' said Julian. 'Then maybe we can let a rope down and get poor Timmy.'

Go to **134**.

149

'I think we should have a really good look all around the castle first,' said Anne firmly. 'It would help us to decide which places to look hardest in.'

The others all stared at the girl. They were not used to Anne having such useful ideas, and they were all rather surprised!

'Let's do that,' said George, jumping to her feet. 'Come on. Oh – wait a minute. Perhaps we should go in pairs – it won't take so long.'

'Good idea,' said Julian. 'George, why don't you go with Dick, and, Anne, you come with me. Be sure to look really well all around the castle, won't you?'

If you want to follow Anne and Julian, go to **125**. *If you want to follow George and Dick, go to* **142**.

'Quick, George,' said Julian. 'Stick your spade under the stone and try to lift it up as we pull.'

George stuck her spade under the edge of the stone, Julian and Dick tugged as hard as they could, and all of a sudden the stone was out! Underneath was . . . nothing! Nothing but earth. The children looked at each other in dismay. All their work had been wasted.

'Oh well,' said Julian. 'Never mind. This stone with the handle must have been put there because they needed a stone and that was the only one they could find.'

'I really thought we'd found the entrance to the dungeons,' said Dick. 'I say, is anyone else hungry? Let's go and have lunch before we do any more looking.'

Go to **146**.

'Let's go on,' said Dick. 'We shall soon find the way out. Hello! What's this?'

They had come to what looked like a chimney shaft of bricks, stretching down from the roof of the dungeon to the floor.

'I know what it is!' said George suddenly. 'It's the well, of course! You remember it was shown in the plan of the dungeons, as well as in the plan of the ground floor. I wonder if there's any opening in it just here, so that water could be taken to the dungeons as well as to the ground floor.'

They went to see. On the other side of the well-shaft was a small opening, big enough for one of them at a time to put his or her head and shoulders through. When they looked up they could see a faint gleam of daylight.

'This is the well, all right,' said Julian. 'And now we've found the well we know that the steps out of the dungeons can't be very far off!'

They hunted a bit further, and then Anne gave a screech of excitement.

'Here's the entrance! It must be, because I can see daylight.'

The children rounded a corner and, sure enough, there was the steep, rocky flight of steps leading upwards. They all went up into the sunshine.

Go to **175**.

152

They all trooped down the tunnel. It was much darker and more mysterious than the wide passage, and at one point Anne gave a shriek as something furry brushed past her ankle.

'It was probably a mouse,' said Julian. He thought it was much more likely to have been a rat, but he didn't want to worry Anne by telling her that!

Soon they came to the end of the tunnel they were in. It made a sort of T-junction with two other tunnels.

'Golly,' said Dick. 'Shall we turn left or right?'

If you think they should turn left, go to **167**. *If you think they should turn right, go to* **158**.

153

Timmy looked very surprised when he found himself being pulled through the air, but he was soon at the top of the well. The children took off the rope, and Julian lowered it back down to George.

'Put it around you under your arms, George,' he called, 'and tie it as firmly as you can. When we start pulling you up, push with your legs against the sides of the well.'

When she was ready, the others all hauled on the rope. Soon George's head appeared at the top of the well.

They dragged her out, and she sat on the ground for a few minutes to recover from her adventure. She had really been rather scared!

'Well, Timmy,' said Dick, 'you shouldn't chase rabbits – but you've certainly done us a good turn, because you've found the well for us. Now we've only got to look around a little to find the dungeon entrance!'

Go to **157**.

A steep flight of steps, cut out of the rock itself, led downwards into darkness. 'Come on!' cried Julian, snapping on his torch. 'We've found what we wanted! Now for the dungeons!'

The steps down were slippery. Timmy darted down first, Julian went after him, then George, then Dick and then Anne. They quite expected to see piles of gold and all kinds of treasure everywhere around them!

It was dark down the steep flight of steps, and it smelt very musty. Anne choked a little.

'I hope the air down here is all right,' said Julian. 'If anyone feels a bit funny they'd better say so and we'll go up into the open air again.'

The steps went down a long way. Then they came to an end. Julian flashed his torch around. A weird sight met his eyes.

The dungeons of Kirrin Castle were made out of the rock itself, and they were very mysterious and full of echoing sounds.

'Isn't it strange?' said George. At once the echoes took up her words, and multiplied them and made them louder. 'Isn't it strange, *isn't it strange, isn't it strange?*'

Julian laughed. 'Come on,' he said. 'Let's explore. Which way shall we go?'

'Look,' said George. 'There's a tunnel. Perhaps the room with the ingots is down there.'

'Or here,' suggested Anne, pointing to the dungeons straight ahead of them.

If you think they should go down the tunnel, go to **168**. *If you think they should explore the dungeons, go to* **159**.

155

'I think we should turn back,' said Anne. 'If we go back to the wooden door we may be able to remember which way we came.'

They turned around and started to try to retrace their steps – but it was no good. The dungeons were very big and rambling, and all the different passages and caves looked almost the same – rocky floors and walls, and here and there old barrels, rotting wood, empty bottles and all sorts of other strange things. At last they came to a very large tunnel, wide and quite smooth.

'This looks like a sort of main passage, with others running off it,' said George. 'Maybe all the prisoners and supplies were brought down here. That's why it's so smooth.'

'In that case,' said Dick, 'it may go to the entrance. I think we should try going along it.'

They all thought this a good idea, so they set off, with Timmy following close behind George, as usual.

Go to **170**.

'Wake up!' she cried to the others. 'Wake up, all of you! It's morning! And we're on the island!'

They all awoke, and were soon having breakfast. Then Julian picked up the axe he had brought and led everyone to the flight of steps. Timmy went too, wagging his tail, but not feeling very pleased at going down into the dark again!

They all went underground once more. And then, of course, they couldn't find the way to the wooden door! It was most tiresome.

'We shall lose our way again,' said George desperately. 'These dungeons are the most rambling, spread-out maze of underground caves and passages I've ever known!'

'Look,' said Julian, taking a piece of chalk from his pocket. 'We can use this. I'll make marks on the walls to show where we've been. That way we shan't get lost.'

So they set off again, Julian marking the wall as they walked along in the musty darkness. Soon they were back at the well.

Go to **180**.

157

If you have arrived from **153**, *score* ⌒ ⌒.

They set to work again to hunt for the dungeon entrance. They dug about with their spades under all the bushes. They pulled up crooked stones and dug their spades into the earth below, hoping that they might suddenly find them going through into space! It was really very thrilling.

They searched for a long time. They knew that the entrance to the dungeons couldn't be far away, but where was it?

If you think that Anne might find it, go to **165**. *If you think that Dick might find it, go to* **160**.

158

'I vote we turn right,' said Dick.

'But surely that will only take us back the way we came,' said George. 'We came down the wide passage from the bottle dungeon, and then we turned off to the right into this passage. If we turn right again we'll only be going back the way we came.'

'Yes, but this passage may turn in a different direction, or go up or down or do anything,' said Dick. 'After all, it must go somewhere!'

'Not necessarily,' argued George. 'It could just lead to a dead end.'

'Oh do stop arguing, you two,' said Anne. 'I think we should do as Dick suggests and turn right.'

So they all started down the passage to the right. George went first, flashing the torch in front of her. They had taken only a few steps down the tunnel when she stopped dead with a shriek.

Go to **173**.

159

If you have arrived from **162**, *score* ◌ ◌ ◌. *If you have arrived from* **178**, *score* ◌ ◌ ◌ ◌.

They moved away from the end of the rocky steps and explored the nearby dungeons. They were really only rocky cellars stretching under the castle.

'I wonder which dungeon was used for storing the ingots,' said Julian. He stopped and took the map out of his pocket. He flashed his torch on it. But although it showed him quite plainly the dungeon where INGOTS were marked, he had no idea at all of the right direction.

'I say! Look – there's a door here, shutting off the next dungeon!' Dick cried suddenly. 'I bet this is the dungeon we're looking for! I bet there are ingots in here!'

Go to **177**.

160

They all went on looking as hard as they could. Suddenly Dick gave an excited shout. 'Look!

Look!' he called to the others. 'Look at this big stone! Here behind this bush. I wonder if this might be it?'

All the others came running over.

'It's so large it might have been put there specially to block the entrance and stop prisoners escaping,' said George. 'Let's see if we can move it.'

The children began to push the big heavy stone, but it refused to budge. They all pushed as hard as they could, but nothing happened.

'We can't move it,' said Anne. 'Oh dear, we can't move it!'

Go to **163**.

161

'Well, I think we should go back and mark the way we went to the wooden door,' said Julian. 'I've got a piece of chalk that we can make marks on the walls with, and it'll save time tomorrow.'

'I'll tell you what,' said George. 'Dick and Anne can start getting the tea, Julian, and you and I can go and mark the route.'

'That's a good idea,' said Dick. 'Get some sticks, Anne, and we'll make a fire and boil the kettle.'

George and Julian went back down the rocky steps at the dungeon entrance, carrying their torches. They started off towards the wooden door, Julian making careful marks on the walls as they went. But they hadn't gone far from the entrance when, even with their torches on, they realised that it was much darker in the dungeons than it had been earlier on.

'I think more light must have come into the dungeons from outside than we realised,' said Julian. He stopped and looked ahead of him.

'You know, George,' he said, 'I think we should go back and wait until the morning. It really is much darker down here now, and it might not be very safe.'

George thought that this was a good idea, so they retraced their steps to the dungeon entrance.

Go to **166**.

162

'I know,' said Julian. 'Let's see if Timmy can find the way. Perhaps he'll remember which tunnel we came out of. Come on, Timmy! You show us the way.'

Timmy ran towards the tunnels and sniffed around the edge of both. Then he set off down the right-hand one. The children followed him and, sure enough, they found themselves back in the very narrow low tunnel that they'd gone through on their hands and knees. Soon they were back at the bottom of the dungeon steps.

Go to **159**.

'Yes, we jolly well can,' said George, gritting her teeth. She was determined not to give up. She had always wondered whether there really were dungeons under her beloved castle, and now she was going to find out!

'Perhaps we could tie a rope around it and pull it out of the way,' suggested Julian. 'It's got quite a rough surface, so I think we could get the rope to stay on.'

Dick ran to fetch the rope, and they tied it around the middle of the big heavy stone.

'Right,' said Julian. 'All together now, pull!'

They all pulled as hard as they could, and bit by bit the stone began to move! All of a sudden it rolled over with a rush, and they all staggered backwards. They dropped the rope and rushed to look.

Underneath where the stone had been was – nothing! Just a patch of earth with a lot of beetles and spiders running about, bewildered by the sudden light.

The children felt very disappointed.

'Oh well,' said Julian, 'we'll just have to keep on looking.'

Go to **165**.

It was very difficult to try to decide which way to go.

'Perhaps we should split up and explore some of the side tunnels,' suggested Dick.

'Supposing two of us got really lost,' said George. 'We'd none of us be able to find each other. Let's explore each tunnel, one by one, and do it all together. That way we'll be together when we find the way back.'

They agreed that this was the best thing to do, so as soon as they came to one of the side tunnels they all went to explore it. The first tunnel they came to ended in a small room that had obviously been used for storage – there were a lot of old barrels and the remains of boxes in it.

'Well,' said Julian, 'this isn't right, that's obvious.'

They went back to the wide main passage and walked on until they came to the next tunnel.

Anne shivered. She was cold and hungry and beginning to be really frightened.

'Oh dear,' she said suddenly. 'Perhaps we'll never get out of here! Perhaps we'll have to spend the rest of our lives down here!'

'Don't be silly, Anne!' said Julian. 'Of course we'll find our way out.' But though he sounded confident, he was really a bit worried himself.

Go to **152**.

If you have arrived from **163**, *score* ⌒◁ ⌒◁.

And then Anne found the entrance! It was quite by accident. She was tired and sat down to rest. She lay on her front and scrabbled about in the sand. Suddenly her fingers touched something hard and cold. She uncovered it – and lo and behold it was an iron ring! She gave a shout and the others looked up.

'There's a stone with an iron ring in it here!' yelled Anne excitedly. They all rushed over to her. Julian dug about with his spade and uncovered the whole stone. Sure enough, it did have a ring in it! Perhaps this stone was the one that covered the dungeon entrance!

Julian tied two or three turns of rope through the ring, and the four of them pulled for all they were worth. The stone moved!

'All together again!' cried Julian. The stone stirred again and then suddenly gave way!

The children fell over in a heap, then Julian and George got to their feet and rushed to the opening that the moved stone had disclosed. They stood there, looking downwards, their faces shining with delight. They *had* found the entrance to the dungeons!

Go to **154**.

*If you have arrived from **161**, score* .

'I think we've done enough for one day,' said Julian. 'I'm ready for tea.'

It was lovely to lie about in the warmth of the evening sun and munch bread and cheese and enjoy cake and biscuits. Timmy ate the titbits the children gave him, and licked George whenever he was near her.

It was past eight o'clock by the time the children had finished their meal and tidied up. Anne was

nearly asleep, she was so tired out with hard work and excitement.

'Come on, Anne!' said George, pulling her to her feet. 'Bed for you. We'll cuddle up together in the rugs on the floor of that little room – and in the morning when we wake we'll be simply thrilled to think of opening that big wooden door.'

All four of them went off to the little stone room and curled up on their piles of rugs. They felt perfectly safe with Timmy on guard.

They slept soundly until the morning, when Timmy saw a rabbit through the broken archway leading to the little room and sped away to chase it. He woke George as he got up from the rugs, and she sat up and rubbed her eyes.

Go to **156**.

167

If you have arrived from **181**, *score* $\bowtie$ $\bowtie$ $\bowtie$.

'Let's turn left,' said George. 'I've a feeling that it's the right way.'

They all turned to the left and started to make their way along the passage. They hadn't gone very far when they came to what looked like a chimney shaft of bricks, stretching down from the roof to the floor. Julian flashed his torch on to it. He was puzzled.

'I know what it is!' said George suddenly. 'It's the well, of course! You remember it was shown in the plan of the dungeons, as well as in the plan of the ground floor? That's the shaft of the well going down and down.'

They all looked around it. On one side of the well was a small opening, big enough for one of them at a time to put his or her head and shoulders through. Julian looked upwards and could see a faint gleam of daylight at the top.

Now that they had found the well they knew that the steps out of the dungeons were not far off. They walked on, rounded a corner, and, sure enough, there was the steep, rocky flight of steps leading upwards. They all went up into the sunshine.

Go to **175**.

168

'Let's explore the tunnel,' said George. 'Come on!'

They all started off down the tunnel, finding their way by the light of Julian's torch. It was chilly and damp, with a strong smell of the sea. The passage had a very rocky floor, and it seemed to slope downwards. Anne felt very nervous, and she stayed close behind Julian. The passage became smaller and smaller, and at one point they had to get down on their hands and knees and crawl along. Timmy made them laugh by the funny way he crept behind George! Soon, however, it became wider and taller again, and they could walk upright.

'Gosh,' said Julian a moment or two later. 'I think it's getting lighter.'

A second or so later they walked into a huge cavern, open to the sea!

Go to **171**.

169

They decided to go straight on. Julian carefully made marks on the walls as they went. They walked for quite a long time without saying anything. Timmy, as usual, trotted just behind George's heels, his tail down. He didn't like the dark and the strange smell in the dungeons.

Suddenly they came out into a wide passage.

'Oh bother!' said George. 'This is the tunnel we found yesterday, the one that leads to the bottle dungeon. We know we don't want to go down there!'

They turned around and walked back the way they had come. Julian carefully rubbed out all the chalk marks he had made. Eventually they found themselves back by the well.

'At least we know where we are now,' said Dick. 'Now – let's try again!' This time when they came to the place where the passage divided, they turned left.

Go to **172**.

Suddenly the tunnel came to a dead end. All they could see, right down near the floor, was a small opening that a man could have crawled through. It seemed to have the remains of a door crumbling away from its hinges. Anne bent down and stuck her head through the little opening.

'Oh!' she said, moving back. 'It's the funniest-shaped dungeon. It looks rather like a bottle! It's got very smooth sides, and I'm sure I can hear the sea not very far away.'

George stared at her.

'I know what it is,' she said. 'It's a bottle dungeon! They used to put poor prisoners in there when the tide was out, and then when it came in the dungeon filled with water and the prisoner was drowned!'

'Oh,' said Anne, 'how beastly! Let's go back the way we came – quickly!'

They all started back up the wide passage.

Go to **164**.

171

The children all stood still in surprise.

'Did you know there was a cave like this on the island, George?' asked Dick.

George shook her head. 'No,' she said. 'It must be hidden by rocks from anyone rowing around the island.'

They walked across the floor of the cave to look at the sea. Sure enough, a large spur of rock stuck out, half concealing the entrance to the cave.

'I expect the sea comes right in when the tide is high,' said George.

'Let's look around the cave and see if there's anything hidden here,' suggested Anne.

They all had a good look around, but there was nothing at all to be seen. The sea had washed away everything except the heaviest stones.

'Well, I suppose we'd better go back to the beginning of the tunnel and start again,' said Dick.

But then they discovered something very strange! They turned to look at the back of the cave to find the entrance to the tunnel, and found that there were not one but two tunnels leading out of the cave!

'Golly,' said Dick. 'Which one did we come out of?'

If you think they came out of the right-hand tunnel, go to **162**. *If you think they came out of the left-hand tunnel, go to* **174**.

172

If you have arrived from **169**, *score* ⌒⊣.

They followed the passage to the left, and it wasn't very long before they found the wooden door.

There it was, stout and sturdy, its old iron nails rusty and red. The children stared at it in delight.

Julian lifted his axe. *Crash!* He drove it into the wood and around about the keyhole. But the wood was still strong, and the axe only went in a couple of centimetres. Julian drove it in once more. The axe hit one of the big nails and slipped a little to one side. A big splinter of wood flew out – and struck poor Dick on the cheek!

He gave a yell of pain. Julian jumped in alarm and turned to look at him. Dick's cheek was pouring with blood!

'Golly,' said Julian, and he shone his torch on Dick. 'Can you bear it a moment if I pull the splinter out? It's a big one, and it's still sticking into your poor cheek.'

But Dick pulled it out himself. He made a face with the pain and then turned very white.

'You'd better get up into the open air for a bit,' said Julian. 'And we'll have to bathe your cheek and stop it bleeding somehow.'

'I'll go with Dick,' said Anne. 'You stay here with George.'

Go to **176**.

173

When George stopped suddenly, they all bumped into each other. Julian knocked George over when he crashed into her. She picked herself up and started to run back the way they had come as fast as she could. The others all ran after her.

'What on earth's the matter?' asked Julian.

George didn't reply.

'Whatever's the matter, George?' said Julian again.

'It was a spider,' said George, panting as she ran. 'The biggest, hairiest one I've ever seen. Hanging down, right in the middle of the passage!'

Go to **181**.

174

'It was the left-hand tunnel,' said Julian. 'I'm sure it was. I remember stubbing my toe on that pile of stones at the entrance as we came out.'

So they set off into the tunnel. They walked along for a short way, and then the tunnel began to slope up a little, and then more and more.

'This isn't the tunnel we came down,' said Anne. 'We came through that bit where we had to go down on our hands and knees.'

'Well, I think we could go on a bit further,' said George. 'I'd like to explore this tunnel. We can always go back to the cave and go down the other tunnel later.'

So they walked on. It was very dark indeed, and the upward slope of the tunnel made it hard work. But then the floor levelled out again, and it was easier to walk.

Then all of a sudden Julian's torch went out, and they were plunged into complete darkness!

Go to **178**.

If you have arrived from **167**, *score* ⌀ ⌀ ⌀ ⌀ .

Once they were all back in the open air, in the yard of the castle, they felt much happier. Julian looked at his watch.

'It's half-past six! *Half-past six!* No wonder I feel hungry. We've been down in those dungeons for hours.'

'Well, let's have a kind of tea-supper before we do anything else,' said Dick. 'I don't feel as if I've had anything to eat for about twelve months.'

'Wait a minute,' said George. 'Don't you think we should go back down to the dungeons and mark the route to the wooden door so that we can find it quickly tomorrow?'

'Oh no,' said Anne and Dick together. 'Let's have tea now!'

If you think they should have tea now, go to **166**. *If you think they should mark the route to the door first, go to* **161**.

176

But Julian thought he would like to see Dick safely up into the open air first. He handed the axe to George. 'You can do a bit of chopping while I'm gone,' he said.

'Right,' said George, and she took the axe.

Julian took Dick and Anne back into the fresh

air. Anne dipped her hanky into the kettle of water and dabbed Dick's cheek gently. The wound wasn't really very bad. Dick's colour soon came back, and he wanted to go down into the dungeons again.

'No, you'd better lie down for a while,' said Julian. 'Your cheek's still bleeding.'

'I'm all right, Julian, I really am,' protested Dick. 'I do want to come back to the dungeons. Supposing you and George find the ingots and Anne and I aren't there? We'd be so disappointed!'

'Well,' said Julian, 'I suppose it's really up to you.'

If you think Dick should stay in the fresh air, go to **185**. *If you think he should go back down to the dungeons, go to* **179**.

177

Four torches were flashed on to the wooden door. It was big and stout, studded with great iron nails. And it was shut fast. No amount of pushing or pulling would open it.

'We'll fetch the axe,' said Julian. 'We may be able to chop around the keyhole and smash the lock.'

'That's a good idea,' said George, delighted.

They left the big door and tried to get back the way they had come. But the dungeons were so big and rambling that they lost their way.

'This is sickening!' said Julian at last. 'I simply haven't any idea at all where the entrance is. What shall we do? Shall we go on down this passage that we're in, or shall we turn back and try again some other way?'

If you think they should keep going, go to **151**. *If you think they should turn back, go to* **155**.

178

Anne gave a shriek of dismay. 'Oh help, it's so dark!'

'All right, Anne, don't worry,' said Julian. 'There's a spare battery in my pocket.'

It wasn't easy changing the battery in complete darkness, but Julian managed it in the end. He turned his torch on again.

'Come on,' said George impatiently. 'Let's get going again.'

In a little while they emerged from the tunnel and found themselves just inside a dungeon. Beside them were some steps.

'Oh look,' said Dick. 'These are the steps down from the entrance. We're back where we started!'

Go to **159**.

179

Dick couldn't bear the thought that the others might find the ingots without him. 'I'm fine,' he insisted, getting to his feet. 'Come on, let's go and see whether George has managed to get the door open!'

They all went back to the dungeon steps.

Go to **188**.

180

'Now,' said Julian, 'whenever we come to the well we shall at least be able to find the way back to the steps, because we can follow my chalk marks. The thing is – which is the way next? We'll try to find it – and I'll put chalk marks all along the walls here and there – but if we go the wrong way and have to come back, we'll rub out the marks and start again from the well another way.'

This was a very good idea. But they hadn't gone far before they came to a place where the passage divided again.

'Oh dear,' said Anne. 'Should we go straight on, or should we bear left?'

If you think they should go straight on, go to **169**. *If you think they should bear left, go to* **172**.

181

George felt very silly admitting that she had run away from a spider. Boys weren't afraid of spiders, and she felt sure that the others would laugh at her.

Anne was relieved she hadn't seen the spider. She wasn't very fond of spiders either, and if George, who was so brave, had been frightened, then it must have been enormous!

Their headlong dash down the tunnel had brought them back to the place where they had wondered whether to turn left or right. They all stopped to get their breath.

'Well, now what shall we do?' said Julian. 'Shall we go back and see if the spider has gone, or shall we go to the left this time?'

Go to **167**.

182

If you have arrived from **203**, *score* ◁ ◁ ◁.

Tim bared his teeth, but the man didn't seem at all frightened of him. He flashed his torch around the dungeon and gave a whistle of surprise.

'Jake! Look here!' he said. 'The gold's here all right – and all in ingots. It will be very easy to take away!'

'You are *not* taking the gold away. It's mine!' said George in a fury.

One of the men laughed. 'You're only a child,' he said. 'You surely don't think you can keep us from getting our way? We're going to buy this island – and everything on it – and we shall take the gold when the deeds are signed. And if by any chance we can't buy the island, we'll take the gold anyway!'

'You will not!' said George. 'I'm going straight home now – and I'll tell my father everything you've said.'

'You are not going anywhere,' said the man. 'Now call this unpleasant dog of yours off, will you?'

If you think that George will call Timmy off, go to **197**. *If you think that Timmy will attack the men, go to* **208**.

183

The room wasn't much more than a cave hollowed out of the rock. But in it was something quite different from the old barrels and boxes the children had found before. At the back were curious, brick-shaped things of dull yellow-brown metal. Julian picked one up.

'George!' he cried. 'The ingots! These are real gold! George, oh George, there's a small fortune here in this cellar – and it's yours! We've found it at last!'

Go to **195**.

184

Julian and George listened as the footsteps faded away down the passage.

'Whew!' said Julian. 'That was a near thing!'

'They said they were going to take the ingots!' said George angrily. 'I'm jolly well going to see that they don't! The ingots are *mine* and nobody's going to take them away! What are we going to do, Julian?'

Julian thought hard. They couldn't move the ingots, because they were very heavy and there were a great many of them, and anyway the men would hear them and come back. Then suddenly he had an idea.

'Listen,' he said to George. 'One of us will have to go and find Dick and Anne and tell them what's happened. Then they can row back to the mainland and tell Uncle Quentin and Aunt Fanny, who can ring the police.'

'But neither of them can row,' objected George. 'Anyway, you know what my father's like. He'd either not listen or he'd think they invented the whole thing. Can't you come up with something else?'

Go to **194**.

185

Dick thought for a minute. He badly wanted to go back to the dungeons with the others, but he still felt a bit odd, even though he had told Julian that he was fine.

'Perhaps you're right, Julian,' he said. 'I'll wait up here for a while.'

'I'll stay with you, Dick,' said Anne. 'Let's go and sit on the rocks over there where we can see the wreck.'

Anne and Dick settled themselves on the rocks, and Julian went back down the dungeon steps.

Go to **191**.

186

'But I can't leave Timmy here,' cried George. 'Goodness knows what might happen to him!'

'He'll follow us,' said Julian. 'Now run! It's our only chance!'

George still hesitated. She couldn't bear to leave Timmy behind with the men. And then suddenly one of them spoke in a menacing voice: 'Call your dog off or I'll shoot him!'

In his hand he held a revolver pointed at Timmy, who was still barking furiously. George caught hold of Timmy's collar and pulled him to her.

'It's all right, Timmy,' she said.

But Timmy knew it was not all right. He continued to growl fiercely.

Go to **205**.

187

Tim stopped barking and began to growl. George looked puzzled.

'Whatever is the matter with Timmy?' she said. 'He surely can't be growling at Dick and Anne?'

Then both children got a tremendous shock, for a man's voice came booming down the dark passage! 'Who's there? Who's down there?'

George clutched Julian in fright. Timmy went on growling, all the hairs on his neck standing up straight.

Julian snapped off his torch, and he and George stood pressed back against the wall of the cellar hardly daring to breathe. And then they saw the beam of a powerful torch coming around the corner of the dungeon passage towards them.

If you think they will be discovered, go to **201**. *If the torch beam misses them, go to* **192**.

188

They hadn't gone more than a few steps underground when Dick suddenly began to feel sick and dizzy. He didn't say anything, and tried to go on walking, but he felt more dizzy with every step he took. He sat down hurriedly on the floor of the cave.

'It's no good, Julian,' he said. 'I think I'm going to faint!'

'Put your head between your knees,' said Julian, who was a Scout and had done some first aid training. 'As soon as you feel a bit better, we'll take you back up into the fresh air.'

After a few minutes Dick started to feel less sick, so Anne and Julian helped him back up the steps into the fresh air.

Go to **193**.

189

Just as Julian was secretly wondering if they hadn't somehow managed to get lost in the big cave, he caught sight of the door in the beam of his torch.

'We're nearly back at the door where we came in,' he said to George.

'And we haven't found anything,' George replied dismally. 'I really did think that we were going to find the ingots in here!'

Julian didn't answer her. He had come to a halt and was shining his torch down towards something by his feet.

'George!' he said. 'Oh George! We *have* found the ingots! Look!'

And there by Julian's feet was a pile of curious brick-shaped objects made of a dull yellow-brown metal.

'They were just by the door all the time,' said George. 'If we'd turned right instead of left when we opened the door, we would have found them straight away!'

'There's a small fortune here in this cellar!' cried

Julian. 'We've found it at last. And it's all yours, George!'

Go to **195**.

190

'I won't,' said George, her face furious. 'I won't get poor Dick and Anne down here to be made prisoners.'

'We shall shoot your dog if you don't do as you are told,' said the first man suddenly.

George's heart sank, and she felt cold. 'No, no,' she said in a desperate voice.

'Well, write the note, then,' said the man,

141

offering her a pencil and paper. 'I'll tell you what to say.'

'I can't,' sobbed George. 'I can't!'

'All right – I'll shoot the dog then,' said the man, and he levelled his revolver at Timmy. George threw her arms around her dog and gave a scream.

'No, no! I'll write the note. Don't shoot Timmy, please don't shoot him!'

Go to **200**.

191

If you have arrived from **193**, *score* ⌒⌒.

Julian followed his chalk marks and soon came to where George was attacking the door. She had smashed it well round the lock – but it simply would *not* give way. Julian took the axe from her and drove it hard into the wood.

After a blow or two something seemed to happen to the lock. It became loose, and hung a little sideways. Julian put down his axe.

'I think somehow that we can open the door now,' he said in an excited voice. 'Now then, push, George!'

They both pushed – and the lock gave way with a grating noise. The door creaked open and Julian and George went inside.

If you think they find anything in the cave, go to **183**. *If you think they don't find anything, go to* **196**.

Julian and George stood frozen to the spot as the torch beam flashed past them. Fortunately it was very dark in the cellar, and as long as the children kept completely still and made no noise, the intruders might not know they were there. Clever Timmy had realised that George wanted him to be quiet and had stopped growling. All three held their breath.

'I don't think there's anyone in here,' said a man's voice.

'I definitely heard a dog barking, and a boy shouted "Dick" and "Anne", and "We've found the ingots". So they're down here somewhere,' said another, gruffer voice.

'We must find them and take care that they don't interfere with our plans to take the ingots,' said the first man. 'Come on, we'd better go and look further down the passage.'

The two men walked out of the cellar.

Go to **184**.

Dick sat down thankfully in the sunshine. He had gone very white again. Julian looked at him anxiously.

'I think you'd better stay here for a while now,' he said. 'You'll soon be fine if you sit quietly for a bit. Anne will stay with you, won't you, Anne?'

'Yes, of course,' said Anne. 'Let's go and sit on the rocks where we can see the wreck.'

Julian saw them settled on the rocks, then he went back down the dungeon steps.

Go to **191**.

194

'Well,' said Julian, 'perhaps Anne and Dick could go straight to the police themselves.'

'The police wouldn't believe them either,' said George, 'but I don't see what else we can do. We've got to stop those men from taking the ingots!'

'You stay here with Timmy,' suggested Julian, 'and I'll go back up to the castle and find Anne and Dick. Will you be all right by yourself?'

'Of course,' said George. 'I've got Timmy.'

But though she spoke bravely she really felt nervous at the idea of being left alone where the two men might find her!

'Oh gosh,' said Julian. 'I've just thought of something. I shan't be able to use a torch to find my way through the passages. If I do, the men will see the beam and know where I am. I'll just have to find my way in the dark! Perhaps I can feel my way along the walls. There's a bit of light coming in here and there, and I may be able to see the chalk marks I made.'

'Good luck!' whispered George, and Julian slipped out of the cellar.

Go to **203**.

If you have arrived from **202**, *score* ◅. *If you have arrived from* **189**, *score* ◅ ◅.

George couldn't say a word. She just stood there, staring at the pile of ingots, holding one in her hands. She could hardly believe that these strange brick-shaped things were really gold. Her heart thumped fast. What a wonderful, marvellous find!

Suddenly Timmy began to bark loudly.

'Shut up, Tim!' said Julian. 'What can you hear? Is it the others coming back?'

He went to the door and yelled down the passage outside. 'Dick! Anne! Is it you? Come quickly, because we've found the ingots! *Hurry! Hurry!*'

Go to **187**.

The room behind the door was a large, lofty cave, dark and echoing. It was so big that they couldn't see the sides as Julian flashed his torch around.

'We'll have to start by the door and feel our way around the walls,' said George, 'to see if we can find anything.'

'I'll put chalk marks on the wall again,' said Julian. 'Then if we come to a tunnel leading out of the cave, we'll be able to find our way back.'

They set off, very carefully feeling their way around the walls of the cave. Julian marked the walls of the cave with his chalk. It was so dark that they could see nothing outside the pool of light from Julian's torch, and they had to move very slowly.

Julian was in front of George, and suddenly he caught sight of something in the beam of the torch.

'Look, George,' he said, pointing his torch ahead of him. 'Over there – I think I can see a sort of archway.'

If you think Julian has seen an archway, go to **202**. *If not, go to* **206**.

197

'No,' said George, 'I won't.'

'I should if I were you,' said the man, and George saw with dismay that he had a revolver in his hand.

'I'll shoot him if you don't,' said the man. 'Now call him off!'

In fright, George caught hold of Timmy's collar and pulled him to her.

'Be quiet, Timmy,' she said. 'It's all right.'

But Timmy knew quite well that it was not all right. He went on growling fiercely.

Go to **205**.

198

'Hey! Where do you think you're going?' said the man with the revolver. 'Don't you try any tricks now! Don't forget we'll shoot your dog if you don't do as we say.'

Jake finished sharpening the pencil and gave it to George. She wrote the note as the man had told her to, and she was just about to sign it when she had a sudden thought. Should she secretly write 'HELP' on the bottom or simply sign the note and hope for the best?

If you think she writes 'HELP', go to **207**. *If not, go to* **214**.

199

If you have arrived from **219**, *score* ◁ ◁.

He took a last look at his mistress, gave her hand a lick, and set off down the passage. Up the rocky steps he bounded and into the open air. Where were Dick and Anne?

He smelt their footsteps and ran off, his nose to the ground. He soon found the two children out on the rocks. Dick was feeling better and was sitting up.

'Hello,' he said in surprise, 'here's Timmy! Did you get tired of being underground in the dark, Tim?'

'Look, Dick,' said Anne, who had sharp eyes, 'he's got something twisted under his collar.'

Go to **216**.

'Write this,' the man told George. '"Dear Dick and Anne. We've found the gold. Come on down at once and see it." Then sign your name, whatever it is.'

George wrote what the man had said. Then she signed her name. But instead of writing 'George' she put 'Georgina'. She knew that the others would feel certain she would never sign her name like that, and she hoped it would warn them that something was up. The man took the note and fastened it to Timmy's collar. The dog growled, but George told him not to bite.

'Now tell him to go and find your friends,' said the man.

Go to **209**.

201

The light picked them out, and the holder of the torch came to a surprised stop.

'Well, well, well!' said a voice. 'Look who's here! Two children in the dungeons of my castle!'

'What do you mean, *your* castle!' cried George.

'Well, it *is* my castle, because I'm in the process of buying it,' said the voice.

Then another voice spoke, more gruffly.

'What are you doing down here? What did you mean when you shouted out "Dick" and

"Anne", and said you had found the ingots? What ingots?'

'Don't answer,' Julian whispered to George. But the echoes took his words and made them very loud in the passage: *'Don't answer! Don't answer!'*

'Oh, so you won't answer,' said the second man, and he stepped towards the children.

Go to **182**.

202

George and Julian felt their way carefully along the wall. Julian shone his torch in front of him to where he thought he could see the archway.

'It *is* an archway,' said George, looking up to the top of the arch, which was a metre or so above their heads. 'There seems to be another cave through there. Let's go and have a look!'

Holding their torches in front of them, they walked cautiously into the next cave. It seemed to be rather small and low. Julian was swinging the beam of the torch around the floor when suddenly it caught something that had a dull glitter. Julian moved closer and looked at a big pile of brick-shaped things of dirty yellow-brown metal.

'George!' he cried. 'The ingots! These are real gold! George, oh George, there's a small fortune here in this cellar – and it's yours! We've found it at last!'

Go to **195**.

Julian inched his way along the passage, his rubber-soled shoes making no sound on the stony floor. At last he reached the bottom of the steps. Just then he heard the sound of men's voices, and Timmy growling.

'Oh no!' he said to himself. 'It sounds as if the men have found George. I'll have to go back and help her.'

He started to retrace his steps, and as he approached the cellar he heard George saying angrily, 'No, I won't answer you!'

'Oh, won't you?' said a man's voice.

As Julian moved towards the entrance the man saw him.

'Here's another one,' he said. 'Come over here and stand beside your friend.'

Go to **182**.

204

'What do you want me to write?' asked George.

'Put this,' said the man. '"Dear Dick and Anne. We've found the gold. Come on down at once and see it." Then sign your name, whatever it is.'

George started to write, but she deliberately pressed so hard that she broke the pencil's lead.

'Oh dear,' she said, holding it up. 'I'm afraid the lead is broken.'

The man called Jake snatched it from her. 'You should have been more careful,' he said angrily. 'Well – I've got a knife. I can easily sharpen it.'

But it took him quite a time to sharpen the pencil, and he had to ask the man with the revolver to hold the torch so that he could see what he was doing. With the torch pointing at Jake, George was for the moment in darkness. Very slowly she began to inch towards the door of the cellar.

Go to **198**.

205

If you have arrived from **186**, *score* ⤴.

'Now listen to me,' said the man with the revolver after he'd had a hurried talk with his companion. 'If you are going to be sensible, nothing unpleasant will happen to you. But if you are obstinate, you will be very sorry. What we are going to do is this – we are going to lock you up here, then take our motor-boat to get a ship and come back for the gold.'

'And you are going to write a note to your companions above, telling them you've found the gold and they are to come down to see it,' said the other man. 'Then we shall lock all of you in this dungeon, with some food and drink, until we get back. Now – write a note to Dick and Anne, whoever they are, and send your dog up with it.'

If you think George does what they ask, go to **210**. *If you think she refuses, go to* **190**.

206

Julian and George felt their way along the wall to where Julian thought he could see the archway.

But when they reached it, and Julian shone his torch over it, they found it was just a shallow recess in the rock. George suddenly felt terribly let down. She was so excited at the idea of finding the ingots that she found any setback very disappointing. She said nothing, though, and went on following Julian around the walls of the cave. It seemed to take a very long time.

Go to **189**.

207

George hesitated for a moment, and then scribbled 'HELP' at the bottom of the note. She knew that the man would look at the note, so she made her writing as small as she could, hoping that he wouldn't spot it.

'Give it to me,' said the man, and he read it through.

'Oh, so you're trying to be clever, are you?' he said.

He tore up the note and gave her another piece of paper.

'Now write the message again,' he said. 'And this time no clever tricks!'

George did as he told her, and then paused.

Go to **214**.

208

Timmy could feel that his beloved mistress did not like the men, and he growled more and more loudly.

'Call him off!' repeated the man.

'No,' said George, 'I won't!'

Timmy started to bark furiously, snarling and baring his teeth at the men. Suddenly he flew at them, forcing them to back against the wall of the dungeon.

Julian seized the chance. 'Come on, George!' he shouted. 'Run!'

Go to **186**.

209

If you have arrived from **214**, *score* ◁ ◁.

'Find Dick and Anne,' commanded George. 'Go on, Timmy. Find Dick and Anne. Give them the note.'

Tim did not want to leave George, but there was something very urgent in her voice. He hesitated for a moment, looking at George with his head on one side as if he was trying to decide what he should do.

If you think Timmy obeys George, go to **199**. *If not, go to* **211**.

210

George stared at the men for a moment, her face furious.

'Go on – or we'll shoot your dog! We mean it,' said the man with the revolver.

'All right,' said George. 'I haven't got any paper or a pencil, though.'

One of the men felt in his pockets and pulled out a diary. Flicking through it he found an empty page and pulled it out.

'Here, use this,' he said.

'But I haven't got a pencil,' said George innocently. She had made up her mind to try to delay writing the note for as long as possible to give Julian time to work out an escape plan.

'Have you got a pencil, Jake?' the man with the revolver said to his companion.

Jake shook his head. 'I don't think so,' he said.

'Here,' said the first man. 'Hold the gun. I've got a pencil in one of my pockets.'

He gave the pencil to George.

'Now write the note!' he said.

Go to **204**.

211

As if making up his mind, Timmy sat down firmly on the floor of the cellar! George almost laughed out loud.

'Go on,' said the man called Jake. 'Send your dog off with the note.'

'He won't go,' said George.

'Well, you'll just have to make him go,' said the other man, 'or else!' And he aimed the gun at Timmy.

Go to **219**.

212

If you have arrived from **240**, *score* ◯.

But all that happened was that the boat went around in circles! Neither Dick nor Anne really knew what they were doing, and they simply couldn't get the oars to move together.

'It's no good,' said Dick, panting. 'You move down the boat, and I'll try on my own.'

Anne clambered very carefully to the end of the boat, and Dick picked up both oars. He got on quite well, and the boat began to move fairly smoothly away from Kirrin Island.

Go to **238**.

213

If you have arrived from **226**, *score* ⌢.

'Look,' said Dick. 'There *is* someone else here. And I bet it's the men who want to buy the island. I bet they've read that old map and know there's gold here. And they've found the other two and want to get us all together down in the dungeons so that they can keep us safe until they've stolen the gold. That's why they made George send us that note, but she signed it with a name she never uses – to warn us!'

Timmy, at the sound of his mistress's name, cocked his head then suddenly turned away and ran off towards the dungeon steps. Dick and Anne stared after him.

'The thing is,' said Dick, 'what are we going to do?'

If you think they should try to row back to the mainland and ring the police, go to **224**. *If you think they should go down to the dungeons, go to* **220**. *If you think they should hide in the little stone room, go to* **218**.

If you have arrived from **207**, *score* ⌒.

She thought for a moment and then signed her name 'Georgina' instead of 'George'. She knew that the others would feel certain she would never sign her name like that, and she hoped it would warn them that something was up. The man took the note and fastened it to Timmy's collar. The dog growled, but George told him not to bite.

'Now tell him to go and find your friends,' said the man.

Go to **209**.

If you have arrived from **223**, *score* ◯⊲.

'The well should be the best place to hide,' said
Dick. 'You'll just not have to mind its being dark.
Come on!'

He picked up a rope, which they would need to
climb down because the ladder wasn't very safe,
and they hurried off to the well. Dick tied the rope
to the top of the old ladder, which was firmly fixed
in the wall. Then he helped Anne into the well and
climbed down himself, slipping the wooden cover
back again over his head as best he could. The old
stone slab that Timmy had fallen on to was still
there. Dick tested it, and it seemed immovable.

'It's safe for you to sit on, Anne,' he whispered.

Anne sat shivering on the stone slab, waiting to
see if they would be discovered or not.

Go to **221**.

216

Dick took the paper from Timmy's collar. He
undid it and read it.

'Dear Dick and Anne,' he read out loud. 'We've
found the gold. Come on down at once and see it.
Georgina.'

'Oooh!' said Anne, her eyes shining. 'They've
found it. Oh Dick – are you well enough to come
now? Let's hurry.'

But Dick didn't get up from the rocks. He sat and stared at the note, puzzled.

'What's the matter?' asked Anne impatiently.

'Well, don't you think it's funny she signs herself Georgina? You know George hates being a girl and having a girl's name. You know she will never answer if anyone calls her Georgina. And yet in this note she signs herself with the name she hates. Almost as if it's a kind of warning that there's something wrong.'

'Oh don't be so silly, Dick,' said Anne. 'What could be wrong? Do come on.'

'Anne, I'd like to pop over to that inlet of ours to make sure that no one else has come to the island,' said Dick. 'Why don't you stay here and keep lookout?'

If you think Anne should stay behind and keep watch, go to **222**. *If you think she should go with Dick, go to* **230**.

217

'I think you'd better stay and keep watch,' said the first man. 'I'll take the food down. Shan't be long.'

Anne and Dick heard one man walk away towards the stone room, while the other one remained in the courtyard, whistling softly.

After what seemed like a very long time the first man came back. Then they heard the two men go off to the cove. Soon afterwards there was the sound of a motor-boat starting up.

Go to **239**.

If you have arrived from **236**, *score* ◁ ◁ ◁. *If you have arrived from* **238**, *score* ◁ ◁ ◁ ◁ ◁.

For the time being the best idea seemed to be to keep out of sight until they could work out what to do.

Dick led Anne to the little stone room where their things were, and they sat down in a corner to think of a plan.

They didn't need to puzzle their brains for very long. The men came up out of the dungeons and began to hunt for the two children! Jake and his companion couldn't imagine why Dick and Anne had not obeyed what George had said in the note and come down to the dungeons!

Go to **227**.

George took hold of Timmy's collar and dragged him through the cellar door into the passage. Timmy promptly sat down again and refused to move.

George looked at him in dismay. He had never disobeyed her before, but it was obvious he could tell there was something wrong.

Suddenly George had an idea. Should she make a dash for the stairs and hope that she would get there before the men knew what she was doing?

But then she realised that she couldn't leave Julian on his own with the men. Goodness knows what might happen to him.

'Go *on*, Timmy,' she ordered, and this time Timmy, hearing the urgent note in her voice, got up.

Go to **199**.

220

They looked at each other in dismay. Anne felt her eyes fill with tears and she started to sniff. She couldn't bear to think of poor Julian and George and Timmy down in the dungeons being threatened by awful men.

'Oh do stop crying, Anne!' said Dick crossly. 'We've got to think hard about the best way to help the others, and crying certainly *won't* help!'

Anne sniffed again once or twice, and then did her best to be brave. But deep down she wished she had never come to Kirrin Island to look for ingots. She said nothing, however, and sat quietly beside Dick while he thought.

'Right!' he said at last. 'This is what we'll do.'

Go to **231**.

221

They heard the men begin to shout for them.

'Dick! Anne! Where are you? The others want you! We've exciting news for you.'

'Well, why don't they let Julian and George come up and tell us then?' whispered Dick. 'I do wish we could find out what's going on.'

The men's voices got louder as they came into the courtyard.

'Where have those kids got to?' said the first man. 'Their boat is still in the cove, so they haven't got away, but we can't wait all day for them. What shall we do?'

Go to **232**.

222

Anne hesitated. She didn't want to be left on her own, but she thought that Dick would be wasting his time going to look at the inlet. She didn't think there could be anything wrong.

'I'll stay here,' she said. 'If Julian and George come up from the dungeons I can tell them where you've gone.'

Dick set off, and Anne sat down again on the rocks. It was very quiet and peaceful, and Anne was beginning to feel rather sleepy when suddenly she heard a sound behind her!

Go to **226**.

223

'Let's try the jackdaw tower,' said Dick.

They tiptoed across the courtyard, keeping a

sharp lookout for the men. Then they crept in behind the bushes and crouched down as low as they could, both holding their breath. But they had forgotten about the jackdaws!

The birds were not used to seeing people on the island, and Anne and Dick disturbed them. They started to fly around the tower, beating their wings and cawing. They made so much noise that Dick was worried.

'I'm sure the men will notice that the jackdaws are upset,' he whispered to Anne, 'and they'll come to see why. Follow me – if we stay here we're bound to be discovered.'

They made their way back to the stone room and peered through the archway again. The men were nowhere to be seen.

Go to **215**.

224

Anne and Dick stared at each other.

'Julian and George must be in desperate trouble,' said Dick. 'We don't know how many men are in the dungeons. That motor-boat is big enough to hold up to six people, I should think.'

'Oh poor George and Julian!' said Anne, and she burst into tears.

'Do stop that, Anne!' said Dick crossly. 'Crying won't help the others. Besides, we've got to think calmly about what we're going to do.'

Anne sniffed once or twice, but she stopped crying and sat quietly beside Dick while he thought furiously. 'Listen,' he said, 'this is what we'll do.'

Go to **229**.

225

'It'll be better if we both take the food down,' said the first man. 'I don't trust that wretched dog.'

'Right,' said the other man.

Listening from down the well, Anne and Dick heard the men walking away.

'Shall we climb out?' whispered Anne.

'Not yet,' said Dick. 'We'll have to wait until they come back from the dungeons. They said they were going back to the mainland in their boat . . . Wait a minute, I've got an idea!'

Go to **237**.

226

Anne sat frozen to the spot, panic-stricken. What if there really was someone else on the island, and they were creeping up on her? She dared not look behind.

Then suddenly a small rabbit scuttled past her across the rocks! Anne gave a huge sigh of relief. She had been sitting so still that the rabbit had come right up to her, and that was what she had heard! She felt very silly, being so frightened of a rabbit, and she made up her mind not to tell any of the others.

Getting to her feet, she decided to follow Dick. She set off around the island and caught up with him at the inlet. He was staring at a small motor-boat that had been pulled up behind their dinghy.

Go to **213**.

227

Dick heard their voices and saw through the broken archway that the men were going in the opposite direction.

'Anne! I know where we can hide!' he whispered excitedly. 'Down the old well! I'm sure no one would ever look there!'

'Oh no, Dick!' replied Anne. 'I couldn't hide in that dark well. Can't you think of somewhere else? I know – what about the bushes at the bottom of the jackdaw tower?'

If you think Anne and Dick should hide in the bushes, go to **223**. *If you think they should hide in the well, go to* **215**.

228

Looking around the beach, he quickly chose a large stone. Feeling in the water by the stern of the boat, he found the propeller. Then he wedged the stone under the propeller. When the men tried to start the boat, the propeller wouldn't move and the boat wouldn't go! Dick ran back to the castle and climbed back down the well to where Anne was waiting.

'I did it!' he said breathlessly.

Dick had got back into the well just in time, for the next minute they heard the men returning from the dungeons.

'Come on, Jake,' said the first man. 'Back to the boat.'

Go to **235**.

229

'We'll have to row back to Kirrin and tell Uncle Quentin and Aunt Fanny what's happened,' said Dick. 'Then they can call the police.'

'But we can't row!' said Anne.

'No,' said Dick, 'but we can try. It can't be *that* difficult, and the sea is perfectly calm today.'

'But George said that there are lots of rocks and currents around the island,' objected Anne. 'What if the boat gets caught on the rocks and smashed? Then we'd all be stuck here!'

'Well, can you think of anything else we can do?' demanded Dick angrily.

Go **234**.

But Anne didn't want to stay there alone. She ran around the coast with Dick, telling him all the time that she thought he was very silly.

However, when they came to the inlet they saw that there was another boat there as well as their own. It was a motor-boat!

Go to **213**.

'We'll go down to the dungeons as quietly as we can,' said Dick, 'and see where the others are. If they're locked up anywhere, we may be able to let them out.'

'But what if the men see us first?' objected Anne. 'They'll catch us and shut us up with Julian and George.'

'Unless we go down into the dungeons, we shan't know for certain that the others *have* been shut up,' said Dick. 'We don't know how many men are down there. In fact, we don't know anything until we go and look, so come on.'

Anne followed her brother down the dungeon steps.

Go to **236**.

'Well, let's take some food and drink down to the two we've locked up,' said the other man. 'Then we'd better go. We can take their boat with us so that none of them can get off the island.'

'Right,' said the first man. 'There's plenty of food and drink in that little stone room. I suppose those kids brought it with them. Come on, we'll go and get some.'

'Hadn't one of us better keep watch?' said the other man. 'In case the other two turn up? Or would it be better if we both take the food down in case those kids and their dog try to make trouble?'

If you think both the men go down to the dungeons with food, go to **225**. *If you think one of them keeps watch, go to* **217**.

233

Anne looked to where Dick pointed. She saw that the two men had piled big, heavy slabs of broken stone over the dungeon entrance. Neither Dick nor Anne could hope to move them.

'Blow!' said Dick. 'How I do hate to think of poor old Julian and George prisoners down below, and we can't help them! Anne – can't *you* think of something to do?'

Anne sat down on a stone and thought hard. She was very worried. Then she brightened up a little and looked at Dick.

'Dick! I suppose ... I suppose we couldn't possibly climb down the well, could we?'

Dick looked at her. 'How?' he asked.

'You know that the well goes past the dungeons, and there's an opening into the dungeons from the well-shaft, because don't you remember that we were able to put our heads and shoulders in and look right up the well to the top? Could we get past the slab that Timmy fell on, do you think?'

'I can try it – but not you, Anne. I'm not going to have you falling down that well. You must stay up here, and I'll see what I can do.'

Go to **243**.

234

'We could go down to the dungeons to see if we can help the others somehow,' suggested Anne.

'Yes, and then *we'd* probably get caught as well!' retorted Dick. 'No! We'll just have to try to get back to Kirrin.'

So they pushed the boat down into the water and jumped in.

'We'll each take an oar,' said Dick. 'If we both row, we should move fast.'

They each picked up an oar and began to row.

Go to **212**.

Dick's attempt to prevent the men from starting their boat was in vain. Before they could use the engine, they had to push the boat further into the water.

'That's odd,' said one of them. 'It feels as if there's something stuck under the propeller.'

Jake felt around the propeller and pulled out the stone Dick had wedged there.

'Look at this!' he said, holding it up. 'One of those dratted kids must have been here!'

'Don't worry about that now,' said the first man. 'Come on, get in!'

Back in the well, Dick and Anne heard the boat start.

'They must have moved the stone,' said Dick. 'Bother! But at least we can get out of the well now. Come on, Anne!'

Go to **239**.

236

They crept along the passage as quietly as they could, straining their ears for any sound. They were quite close to the cellar door when they heard voices.

'If those kids don't come down to look for their friends soon, we'll have to go and look for *them*,' said a man's voice. 'The dog came back without the note, so they should have been here by now.'

'We'll lock these two in here and go and look for the others,' said another voice.

'Come on, Anne,' whispered Dick. 'We can't stay here!'

They went back to the dungeon steps as quickly and quietly as they could.

'Now what are we going to do?' asked Anne when they were back in the castle.

If you think they should try to row to the mainland, go to **240**. *If you think they should hide in the little stone room, go to* **218**.

237

'What is it?' asked Anne.

'If I can get to their boat and damage it in some way before they come back up from the dungeons, they won't be able to get away!'

'Yes,' said Anne with a shiver. 'Only then they'll be stuck here on Kirrin Island with us! I don't like that idea!'

'But if we don't get back to Kirrin Cottage when we said we would, Aunt Fanny and Uncle Quentin are bound to come and look for us, and then the men will get caught,' replied Dick. 'Anyway, it's worth a try!'

Climbing up the rope, he pushed the wooden cover aside and looked cautiously over the top of the well. The courtyard was empty, so he climbed out and ran as fast as he could to the inlet.

Go to **242**.

238

But soon Dick was finding it harder and harder to make any progress. In fact, he was sure they were going towards the island, not away from it!

'We don't seem to be moving very far,' said Anne.

'No,' said Dick. 'I think we're going back towards the island, not away from it. We must be caught in one of the currents that George told us about.'

Sure enough, despite Dick rowing as hard as he could, they soon found themselves back in the little inlet! The bottom of the boat bumped gently on the sand, and Anne and Dick got out and pulled the boat up the beach again.

'What shall we do now?' asked Anne.

Go to **218**.

239

If you have arrived from **246**, *score* 🔁 🔁 🔁. *If you have arrived from 235, score* 🔁 🔁 🔁 🔁.

Anne and Dick climbed out of the well and stood in the sunshine for a minute to get warm. It had been

very cold in the well. They could see the motor-
boat streaking towards the mainland.

'Well, they've gone for the moment,' said Dick.
'And they've not taken our boat after all. If only we
could rescue Julian and George we could get help,
because George could row us back.'

'Why *can't* we rescue them?' asked Anne. 'We
can go down the steps and unbolt the door, can't
we?'

'No, we can't,' said Dick. 'Look!'

Go to **233**.

'We can't stay here,' said Dick, 'because those men said they'd be coming to look for us. We'll have to try to row back to Kirrin for help.'

'But we can't row!' protested Anne.

'Well, we've jolly well got to try,' said Dick. 'Now come on!'

They ran back to the inlet and climbed into the boat. Each taking an oar, they began to row.

Go to **212**.

241

After a while Dick came to the door of the store-room. As he expected, it was fastened so that Julian and George couldn't get out. Big bolts had been driven home at the top and bottom.

Julian and George were sitting inside the store-cave feeling angry and exhausted. They hadn't touched the food and drink the men had brought them. Timmy was with them, lying with his head on his paws.

'I wonder what the others are doing?' said George. 'At least they had the sense to realise that there was something wrong when I signed that note "Georgina" and not "George". Why – what's the matter, Timmy?'

Timmy suddenly gave a growl. He leapt to his feet and went over to the door, listened for a moment, and then started to wag his tail!

Dick's voice called to them: 'Hi, Julian! Hi, George! Are you there?'

'Dick! Dick! Can you open the door?' called Julian.

'Hold on a minute and I'll try!' shouted Dick. 'I say, these bolts seem awfully stiff! I'm not sure I can undo them.'

'Keep trying!' said George urgently.

'Or you could look for something to hit them with,' suggested Julian.

Should Dick go on trying to undo the bolts? If so, go to **257**. *If you think he should go to find something to hit them with, go to* **261**.

242

The men's boat was sitting on the beach, its stern in the water. Dick looked at it. He didn't know very much about boats, and wished that George had been there as she would have known exactly what to do with it! He thought of trying to smash the engine, but it looked too solid and strong. Besides, he knew that it could be dangerous to meddle with an engine – he could end up getting hurt himself. He racked his brains, knowing that time was short. If he didn't leave the beach soon, the men might catch him there.

If you think Dick tries to do something to the boat, go to **288**. *If you think he decides it's safer to leave the beach right away, go to* **246**.

'Be careful, won't you?' said Anne anxiously.

'Don't worry,' replied Dick as he lowered himself over the edge of the well. 'I'll be all right.' He took a firm hold of the rope, which was still attached to the top of the ladder. Gradually he let himself down until he reached the stone slab.

He tried to squeeze past it, but it was very difficult. At last he managed it, and went on down, half clinging to the rope, half using the ladder.

But before he could reach the opening to the dungeons, the rope ran out.

Go to **249**.

244

When they got to the inlet, a thankful sight met their eyes. There was the boat, lying where they had pulled it out of reach of the waves. But what a shock for them!

'They've taken the oars!' said George in dismay. 'The beasts! They know we can't row the boat without oars. Now we're stuck. We can't possibly get away!'

Go to **255**.

If you have arrived from **267**, *score* ⌒.

'But what about Timmy?' said George. 'We'll never get him up the well-shaft, and you say the dungeon entrance is blocked with stones.'

'I'm afraid we'll just have to leave him down here,' said Julian. 'We'll rescue him later.'

George turned on him. 'How can you suggest such a thing? I can't possibly leave Timmy behind. If he stays, I stay!'

It took Dick and Julian quite a time to persuade George that she should go with them up the well-shaft. But at last she put her arms around the dog and said to him: 'It's only for a little while, Timmy. You'll be all right, really you will.' Then, without looking back, she followed the others through the hole in the well-shaft.

It wasn't long before they were all up in the open air once more, giving Anne hugs and hearing her exclaim how pleased she was to see them all again.

Go to **251**.

246

Dick was too worried that the men might come down to the beach and find him if he stayed there any longer. He was also worried about poor Anne, who was still in the well and probably getting rather frightened. So he went back to the castle and climbed down the well again. He was in the nick of time, because he had just put the well cover back when he heard the men come up from the dungeons and go off to the cove. Then Anne and Dick heard the sound of the motor-boat starting up.

'Right!' said Dick. 'Out we get!'

Go to **239**.

247

'What's the matter?' asked Julian. 'The boat looks all right to me. They haven't made a hole in it or anything.'

'No,' answered George, 'but they've taken the oars. We can't go anywhere without them!'

Go to **255**.

248

When they had finished eating, Julian got to his feet.

'Come on,' he said. 'We'd better go and fix that rope on the dungeon steps before the men come back, and then we'll all have to hide nearby so that we can block the entrance again as soon as they've gone down.'

George ran back to the little stone room where they had left their supplies to get a thin rope, and then joined the others, who were trying to move the stones the men had piled over the dungeon entrance.

'Goodness!' said Anne, after a few minutes. 'I don't think we're going to be able to move these stones!'

Go to **253**.

249

Dick clung to the end of the rope, his feet perched on the ladder. Should he risk going on down the ladder? At this particular point it felt quite strongly attached to the well, but it might be less safe further down. Of course, the quickest way would be to go on down the ladder, if it would hold him, and he did want to rescue Julian and George as soon as possible.

On the other hand, he could play safe. He could tie the end of the rope to the ladder, then call up to Anne and ask her to untie it at the top and drop it down to him.

What should he do?

If you think Dick should use the rope, go to **254**. *If you think he should use the ladder, go to* **258**.

250

They waited for a few minutes to give the men plenty of time to get up to the castle, then they ran softly and swiftly to the old courtyard. They saw that the stones had been pulled away from the entrance to the dungeons. The men had disappeared. They had plainly gone down the steps.

'Come on,' said Julian. 'Let's try and put those stones back.'

But they couldn't move any of the very big stones. They put three smaller ones across, and Julian hoped that the men wouldn't be able to move them from below.

Just as they had finished, they heard a whining noise.

'Timmy!' exclaimed George.

They moved back one of the stones and Timmy squeezed through to a joyful reunion with his delighted mistress.

'Now – if only Dick has managed to bolt them into that room!' said Julian.

Go to **260**.

251

'Now come on!' said George after a minute. 'Off to the boat. Quick! Those men may be back at any time.'

'They might have taken our boat with them,' suggested Julian.

'No,' said Dick. 'Anne and I heard them talking, and they said that they were going to take our boat. But we saw them leaving and they weren't towing it, so it should still be there.'

'But maybe they set it adrift,' said George.

'Or they might have tampered with it some-how,' added Julian.

'Oh, I do hope not!' said Anne.

They ran to the inlet, very worried about whether the boat would be there or not.

If you think the boat has been set adrift, go to **256**. *If you think it's still on the beach, go to* **244**.

252

Down in the dungeons the two men, and another man who was now with them, had expected to find Julian and George still locked up in the store-room with the ingots. They passed the well-shaft, not guessing that a boy and a dog were nearby, ready to slip out as soon as they had passed.

Dick heard the men. He slipped out and followed them quietly, his feet making no sound. He held tightly to Timmy's collar, praying that the dog would stay quiet. Before long he realised that it would be better to let Timmy escape, so with an urgently whispered 'Find George!' he let the dog go. Timmy raced towards the dungeon steps.

Dick had not followed the men very far before he heard one of them exclaim in annoyance.

'Blast these passages! I don't remember which one we went along to find the cave with the ingots in it. Do you know which one it is, Jake?'

They were standing at a place where the passages met in a sort of crossroads.

To the right was a high, narrow passage, to the left a very wide passage, and straight on was a passage with a square-shaped rock to one side of it.

'I haven't a clue which is the right one,' said the man called Jake. 'Anyone got any ideas?'

If you think they should turn right, go to **264**. *If you think they should turn left, go to* **269**. *If you think they should go straight on, go to* **277**.

253

The others soon found that Anne was right! No matter how hard they tried, they still could not lift the large slabs of rock that the men had piled over the dungeon entrance.

'It's no good,' panted Julian. 'We can't move them. We'll just have to go back to the cove and wait until the men come back, then Dick can go down to the dungeons and try to bolt them in.'

So they went wearily back to the cove and settled down to wait. George felt rather upset. She was very worried about Timmy, alone in the dungeons in the dark. They had heard him barking while they were trying to move the stones, and she knew he must be wondering where she was.

After about two hours they saw a big fishing-smack appear in the distance, and heard the *chug-chug-chug* of a motor-boat, too.

Go to **262**.

If you have arrived from **258**, *score* ⌢.

'Anne!' he shouted. 'Anne! Can you hear me?' His voice sounded far-off and funny to Anne, who was waiting anxiously at the top of the well.

'Yes, I can!' she called back.

'The rope's run out,' shouted Dick. 'Can you untie your end of the rope and let it down? I'm tying this end to the ladder.'

'Yes, all right,' replied Anne.

She leant over the edge of the well and started to undo the knot at the top of the rope, but she realised in dismay that it had been tied so tightly that it would be very difficult to get it undone.

'What's the matter?' called Dick. 'Why is it taking you so long?'

'I can't get the knot undone,' replied Anne, nearly in tears.

'Well, don't give up,' shouted Dick. 'If you keep on working away at it, it'll come undone.'

At last Anne felt the knot begin to loosen. It took only a moment after that for her to untie the rope and let it fall down to where Dick was waiting.

'Thanks, Anne!' he called, knotting the rope firmly to the ladder. Then he shouted: 'Right, I'm going on down!'

Go to **265**.

If you have arrived from **247**, *score* ⌢.

It was a great disappointment. After Dick's marvellous rescue of Julian and George, it had seemed as if everything was going right – and now suddenly things were going wrong again.

'We must think this out,' said Julian. 'The men have probably gone to get a ship in which they can put the ingots and sail away. You can't charter a ship in a hurry, so they won't be back for some time – unless, of course, they've got a ship of their own.'

'And in the meantime all we can do is sit here and wait patiently until the men come back and take my gold!' said George.

'You know, I might have a plan,' said Julian thoughtfully. 'Don't interrupt me for a while – I'm thinking.'

Go to **263**.

256

The boat had gone! Then Dick gave a shout: 'There it is!'

Sure enough, there was the boat bobbing merrily a short distance off the beach. George gave a sigh of relief.

'Phew!' she said. 'They obviously pushed the boat into the water, meaning it to float away, but the funny currents around the island have brought it back again.'

Rolling up the legs of their jeans, she and Julian waded out and pulled the boat in.

'Now we can get back to Kirrin,' said Anne thankfully.

'Oh no, we can't,' said George grimly. 'Look!'

Go to **247**.

257

Dick finally managed to unbolt the door at top and bottom and fling it open. He rushed in and thumped Julian and George happily on the back.

George grinned at Dick. 'Good work!' she said. 'What happened?'

Dick told them in a few words all that had taken place.

'You're a brick!' said Julian. 'A real brick! Now come on – let's get out of here!'

Go to **245**.

258

Dick decided to carry on down the ladder and trust to luck. He just hoped the ladder wouldn't give way and plunge him to the bottom of the well!

The ladder seemed perfectly safe – but then all of a sudden it came to an end, broken right off. Dick looked around for the opening to the dungeons, but could see nothing. It must still be some way below him.

'Blow!' he said to himself. 'I'll have to use the rope after all.'

He climbed carefully back up the ladder until he reached the end of the rope.

Go to **254**.

259

The children talked things over, and in the end decided that it would be best to use the trip rope. Nobody really liked the idea of one of them having to be stuck in the dungeons, even with Timmy there. Then George said she thought it would be a good thing to have a meal. They were all feeling very hungry after all their worry and excitement.

They fetched some food from the little room and ate it in the cove, keeping a sharp lookout for the return of the two men.

Go to **248**.

260

The three children went back to the well. Dick had removed the old wooden cover, and it was lying on the ground. The children leaned over the hole and waited anxiously. They knew Dick would have to

come up there now that the entrance was blocked.
What was Dick doing? They could hear nothing
from the well and they longed to know what was
happening.

In fact, there was plenty happening down
below!

Go to **252**.

261

It was frustrating to be so close to being rescued
and to know that Dick was just the other side of the
door. Julian and George started to push against
the door with their shoulders, but it was old and
heavy and thick, and wouldn't move.

Suddenly Dick called to them: 'Hang on a
minute!'

There was silence on the other side of the door
for a little while, and then Dick's voice spoke again:
'I think I can deal with these bolts now!'

Go to **267**.

262

If you have arrived from **253**, *score* ⌢ ⌢.

'There they are!' said Julian in excitement, and he
jumped to his feet. 'That's the ship they mean to
load with the ingots – and there's the motor-boat

bringing the men back. Quick, Dick, down to the dungeons with you!'

Dick shot off to the well, feeling rather nervous but comforted by the thought that Timmy would be with him. Julian turned to the others.

'We'll have to hide,' he said. 'Now the tide is out we can go over there, behind those uncovered rocks.'

The three of them hid themselves behind the rocks, and soon they heard the motor-boat come chugging into the tiny harbour. They could hear voices, and there seemed to be more than two men this time. Then the men left the inlet and went up towards the castle.

Go to **250**.

263

The others waited in silence while Julian sat and frowned, thinking of his plan. Then he looked at them with a smile.

'Listen,' he said. 'We'll wait here until the men come back. What will they do? They'll drag away those stones at the top of the dungeon entrance and go down the steps. They'll go to the store-room where they left us, thinking we'll still be there, and they'll go into the room. Well, what about one of us being hidden there ready to bolt *them* into the room? Then we can either go off in their motor-boat or our own boat, if they bring back the oars, and get help.'

Anne thought it a marvellous scheme, and Dick bravely suggested that he should be the one to hide in the dungeons. But George wasn't so certain that it was a good idea.

'We'll have to go down and bolt the door again to make it seem as if we're still in there,' said George. 'And suppose Dick, or whoever hides down there, can't keep Timmy quiet, or doesn't manage to bolt the men in? They'll simply catch him and come up to look for the rest of us!'

Go to **270**.

264

If you have arrived from **281**, *score* ◁◁ ◁◁.

'Let's try this one,' said one of the men, pointing to the high, narrow passage. 'I think it looks familiar.'

The men set off down the passage with Dick following behind them, his heart thumping loudly. But the men hadn't gone very far before a strong smell of the sea filled the passage, and the passage began to slope downwards. The roof of the passage became lower and lower. Dick kept well back. He knew that this wasn't the way to the store-cave where the ingots were, and he thought the men would soon realise that they were going the wrong way and turn back. He didn't want to be too close to them when that happened!

Go to **272**.

265

Dick moved cautiously down the well. He seemed to have gone a long way before he at last came to the gap in the well-shaft. The little hole had obviously been used by people in the dungeons to get water out of the well. Dick managed to catch hold of the edge, and then scrambled through the opening into the dungeons.

He could now follow the chalk marks to the room or cave where the ingots where – and where he felt sure Julian and George were imprisoned!

He put his head back into the shaft and yelled at the top of his voice: 'Anne! I'm in the dungeons! Watch out that the men don't come back!'

Then he began to follow the white chalk marks.

Go to **241**.

266

The children talked things over, and in the end decided that it would be best if Dick went down to the dungeons to try to bolt the men in the store-room.

'Of course, with Timmy still down in the dungeons,' said George, 'Dick won't be entirely on his own.'

Anne thought it would be a good thing to have a meal. They were all feeling very hungry after their worry and excitement.

They fetched some food from the little room and ate it in the cove, keeping a sharp lookout for the return of the two men. After about two hours they saw a big fishing smack appear in the distance and heard the *chug-chug-chug* of a motor-boat, too.

Go to **262**.

267

George and Julian heard a tremendous banging on the door. Dick was obviously hitting the bolts with something.

All of a sudden the door was flung open, and Dick rushed into the store-cave.

'Good work!' said George. 'What did you hit the bolts with?'

'I found a large stone,' replied Dick. Then he told them in a few words all that had happened.

'You're a brick!' said Julian. 'A real brick! Now come on – let's get out of here!'

Go to **245**.

268

The first man swung his torch around and gave a loud exclamation.

'The children have gone! How strange! Where are they?'

Two of the men were now in the cave – and the

third stepped in at that moment. Dick darted forwards and slammed the door. He fumbled with the bolts, his hand trembling. They were stiff and rusty. He found it hard to shoot them home in their sockets. And meanwhile the men weren't idle!

As soon as they heard the door slam, they spun around. The third man put his shoulder to the door at once and heaved hard, just as Dick had got one of the bolts almost into its socket. Then all three men forced their strength against the door, and the bolt started to give way!

Dick stared at it in horror, then frantically struggled to get the other bolt done up before the men could get out.

If you think Dick succeeds in bolting the men in, go to **274**. *If not, go to* **285**.

269

If you have arrived from **272**, *score* ◁ ◁.

The men discussed which way to go, and then decided to take the wider passage. The floor was very smooth, as if it had been worn down by many years of use.

Dick followed the men a little way behind, his heart thumping so loudly he felt sure that the men must hear it! He strained his ears to hear what they were saying.

'This looks like the right passage,' said one of the

men. 'It's obviously been used a lot. The door to the store-cave must be along here somewhere.'

Go to **281**.

270

'That's true,' said Julian thoughtfully. 'Well – supposing that did happen. While they are down there we could pile some stones back over the dungeon entrance to prevent the men coming up. Dick could escape up the well-shaft. The men don't know about that.'

But George was still not happy with the idea.

'Have you got a better idea, then?' asked Dick.

George thought for a moment.

'I know!' she said excitedly. 'We could stretch a rope across the dungeon steps to trip them up as they go down. They'll fall to the bottom of the steps, and we can pile stones over the entrance to stop them getting out again. And none of us will be stuck down in the dungeons waiting for them. We can let Timmy out at the same time.'

Julian looked at Anne and Dick.

'Which plan should we use?' he asked.

If you think they should try the trip rope, go to **259**. *If you think Dick should try to bolt the men into the store-room, go to* **266**.

If you have arrived from **283**, *score* ◁ ◁.

Unluckily for Dick, the men had just caught sight of him as he vanished into the well-shaft. Suddenly a torch was flashed on to him as he clung to the rope.

'So there you are!' said Jake. 'Thought you could lock us in, did you? We don't think that's very funny, you know.'

He sounded so menacing that Dick felt cold all over.

'Now you come out of there!' ordered Jake. 'Or I'll come in and get you.'

'No!' said Dick.

'All right, then,' said Jake, and he started to climb through the opening.

Go to **282**.

Sure enough, before they had gone much further Dick heard an angry voice: 'This certainly isn't the way! We didn't come down a passage this narrow!'

'No, we didn't,' agreed one of the others. 'Come on, we'd better go back to where the passages cross each other.'

Dick flattened himself into a shallow recess in the passage wall. He was scared that the men's torchbeam would pick him out, but they went past without seeing him.

Leaving a good distance between himself and the men, Dick followed them back to where the passages crossed.

'Now where?' said Jake.

Ahead of them was the very wide passage. To their right was the passage with the pile of rocks. The left turn, they knew, would lead them back to the dungeon entrance.

If you think they should go straight on, go to **269**. *If you think they should turn right, go to* **277**.

273

George just made it to the rowing-boat in time. The others had already pushed the boat out on to the water, and George grabbed the oars and pulled for all she was worth.

The three men ran to their motor-boat. Then they paused in the greatest dismay – for George had completely ruined it! She had chopped wildly with her axe at all the machinery she could see, and now the boat couldn't possibly be started!

'You wicked girl!' yelled Jake, shaking his fist at George. 'Wait until I get you!'

'I'll wait!' George shouted back, her blue eyes shining dangerously. 'And you can wait too! You won't be able to get off my island now!'

Go to **280**.

Just in time, Dick's trembling fingers pushed the bolt home and he sank down against the wall of the passage, shaking all over and trying to catch his breath.

Angry shouts were coming from inside the store-cave.

'Hey, you! Let us out of here, do you hear, or it'll be the worse for you when we catch you! Let us out!'

Dick laughed. 'No, I jolly well won't!' he called back. 'You can stay there until the police come and let you out!'

And he started back down the corridor to the well-shaft, to go and tell the others that the men were locked up and they could all go back to Kirrin and get help.

And then he heard a banging noise!

Go to **279**.

275

If you have arrived from **282** *or* **283**, *score* $\bigcirc\!\!\!\!\!\wedge$ $\bigcirc\!\!\!\!\!\wedge$.

Dick heard the sound of footsteps fading away. Trembling from head to foot, he began to climb the rope he had left dangling from the bottom of the ladder. He squeezed around the stone slab near the top and clambered out. The others were there waiting for him.

'It was no good,' said Dick, panting with his climb. 'I couldn't do it. They burst the door open and chased me. I got into the shaft just in time.'

'They're trying to get out of the entrance now!' cried Anne suddenly. 'Quick! What shall we do? They'll catch us all!'

'To the boat!' shouted Julian, and he took Anne's hand to help her along. 'Come on! It's our only chance! The men may be able to move those stones.'

The four of them fled from the courtyard. George darted into the little stone room as they passed it and picked up an axe.

Go to **288**.

276

Julian, Dick and Anne stared at Jake in horror.

'Surely he won't shoot George, will he?' muttered Dick.

'I don't think so,' said Julian. 'He's just trying to frighten us.'

But secretly Julian wasn't so sure. He knew that the men were desperate and would do anything to get the gold for themselves.

'What are we going to do?' asked Anne. 'Oh Julian – what are we going to do?'

'I suppose we'll just have to do as they say and go back to the shore,' said Julian. It was sickening to think that the men might beat them after all!

But just as they started to pull the boat back to the shore, something unexpected happened!

Go to **284**.

277

If you have arrived from **272** *or* **281**, *score* ⌒ᗡ ⌒ᗡ.

The men decided to take the passage that had a square-shaped rock at its entrance. Dick still followed, keeping well beind. Soon they turned into the wide passage where the store-cave lay.

'Here it is,' Dick heard one of them say as he flashed his torch on the great door. 'The gold's in there – and so are the kids!'

Dick was glad that he had just had time to slip along and bolt the door again before hiding in the well, otherwise the men would have known that Julian and George had escaped, and be on their guard.

The first man opened the door and stepped inside. The second man followed him. Dick crept as close as he dared, waiting for the third man to go in too. Then he planned to slam the door and bolt it!

Go to **268**.

278

If you have arrived from **295**, *score* ⌒ᗡ.

Their little boat reached land. The children leapt

198

out into the shallow water and dragged it up to the beach. Timmy pulled at the rope too, wagging his tail. He loved to join in anything the children were doing.

'Will you take Timmy to Alf?' asked Dick.

'I'm not sure,' said George, looking worried. 'We haven't any time to waste, but I don't know what my parents will say if they see Timmy. I suppose I could leave him tied up to the boat for a little while. Oh dear, I wonder what I should do?'

If you think George should leave Timmy on the beach, go to **292**. *If you think she should take him home, go to* **289**.

279

The men were trying to break down the door! They were pushing against it with their shoulders. The top bolt wasn't very strong, and it gave way quite quickly, but the bottom bolt refused to budge.

Dick walked back to the door and looked at it in horror. He didn't know whether the bottom bolt was strong enough to hold the door closed, and he looked around frantically for something to prop against the door to hold it shut, but he couldn't see anything that would do.

Suddenly the men stopped battering at the door. Dick hoped they'd given up, but they hadn't.

Go to **283**.

If you have arrived from **284**, *score* ⌒⌒ ⌒⌒.

The three men stood at the edge of the sea, watching George pull strongly away from the shore. They could do nothing. Their boat was quite useless.

'The fishing-smack they've got waiting out there is too big for that little inlet,' said George. 'They'll have to stay there until someone goes in with a boat. I guess they're as wild as can be!'

Their boat had to pass fairly near the big fishing-boat. A man hailed them as they came by.

'Ahoy there! Have you come from Kirrin Island?'

'Shall we ignore him?' Dick asked Julian.

'Yes – oh, wait a minute! Perhaps we should tell him some tale that might make him go away. Then the men on the island would be really stuck!' said Julian. 'What do you think, George? What should we do?'

If you think the children should ignore the man in the fishing-boat, go to **286**. *If you think they should tell him a tale, go to* **290**.

Suddenly the tunnel came to a dead end. All they could see, right down near the floor, was a small opening that a man could only just have crawled through. It seemed to have the remains of a door, crumbling away on its hinges.

'Well, this certainly isn't it!' said Jake angrily. 'Now where do we go?'

'Back to where the tunnels cross each other, I suppose,' said one of the other men, and they began to retrace their steps. Dick stepped into the mouth of one of the passages that led off to the side, and flattened himself against the wall as the men went past. Then he followed them back to the place where the passages crossed.

Straight ahead lay the high, narrow passage, while the passage with the square-shaped rock was to their left.

'We can't turn right,' said one of the men, 'or we'll end up back at the steps. But should we go straight on, or turn left?'

If you think they should go straight on, go to **264**. *If you think they should turn left, go to* **277**.

282

But Jake couldn't get through the gap! It was too small. Try as he might, he couldn't reach Dick.

'Look here, Jake!' said the first man, 'we're wasting time. Let's go back to the cave and get the gold. We don't need to worry about these kids. They won't be able to stop us getting away from the island with the ingots.'

'That's right,' said the third man. 'Let's just grab the gold and get out of here!'

Go to **275**.

283

Suddenly there was the sound of hard objects being hurled at the door! At first Dick thought that they were throwing stones at the door to try to smash a hole in it, but then he realised that it must be the ingots they were using! Gold ingots are very heavy, and it wasn't long before a crack appeared in the centre of the door. It quickly grew to a large hole.

Dick stared at the door for a moment, frozen with fear, and then took to his heels and fled down the passage to the well-shaft. Quickly he climbed inside. He could hear the men coming after him, and huddled against the side of the well, waiting for a torch to be flashed into the well and the men to find him.

If you think the men find Dick, go to **271**. *If you think they don't see him, go to* **275**.

284

Timmy suddenly jumped off the bow of the rowing-boat, where he had been standing, and flew towards Jake. He had been wanting to bite Jake for a long time, and this time he was determined to do it! It was obvious to Timmy that his beloved mistress was in trouble, and he had to help her.

With a tremendous snarl Timmy sank his teeth into Jake's leg as hard as he could. Jake gave a yell and dropped the gun. He began to dance up and down, trying to make Timmy let go of his leg. But Timmy hung on grimly. George seized her chance and ran like mad to the boat. She jumped in and began to row.

'Come on, Timmy!' she called.

Timmy let go of Jake's leg with some regret and ran back to the boat.

'Oh well done, Timmy!' said Anne, patting the dog all over. 'You are a clever dog!'

'You wicked girl!' yelled Jake from the shore. 'Wait until I get you!'

'I'll wait,' said George, her blue eyes shining. 'And you can wait, too! You won't be able to leave my island now!'

Go to **280**.

285

But he couldn't get the bolt closed in time. The door started to open, and Dick turned and fled down the passage. The men flashed their torches on and saw him. They went after him at top speed.

Dick fled to the well-shaft. Fortunately the opening was on the opposite side, and he thought he could clamber into it without being seen in the light of the torches. He shot into the opening just as the men came running up to the well-shaft.

'Hey, you! Come back here!' he heard one of them shout.

Dick huddled inside the well, waiting for a torch to be flashed into the well and the men to find him.

If you think the men find Dick, go to **271**. *If you think they don't see him, go to* **275**.

286

'Let's just ignore him,' said George.

'*Ahoy there!*' yelled the man angrily. 'Are you deaf? Have you come from the island?'

The children said nothing at all, but looked away while George rowed steadily. The man on the ship gave up and looked in a worried manner towards the island. He felt sure the children had come from there, and he knew enough of his comrades' adventures to wonder if everything was all right on the island.

'He may put a boat out from the smack and go to see what's happening,' said George. 'Well, he can't do much except take the men off – with a few ingots! I hardly think they'll dare to take any of the gold, though, now that we've escaped to tell our tale!'

Julian looked behind at the ship. He saw a little boat being lowered into the sea.

'You're right, George,' he said. 'They're going to rescue those three men. What a pity!'

Go to **278**.

287

She found Uncle Quentin at his desk.

'What is it, Fanny?' he said irritably.

'Quentin, I think you should come back and hear what the children have to say,' she said. 'I'm sure that something important has happened. I don't think Anne could have invented all the things she just said to me.'

'Really, Fanny, can't you see how busy I am?' he replied. 'I haven't got time to listen to silly stories.'

'I think you should come and talk to the children,' repeated Aunt Fanny.

'Oh, very well,' said Uncle Quentin. 'Bring them in!'

Aunt Fanny went to call the children.

'Now,' said their uncle when they had settled themselves, 'what is all this about?'

Go to **297**.

288

The children dashed down to the cove, with Timmy barking madly. Their own boat lay there without oars. The motor-boat was there too. George jumped into it and gave a yell of delight.

'Here are our oars!' she shouted. 'Take them, Julian. I've got a job to do here! Get the boat down to the water, quickly!'

Julian and Dick took the oars. Then they dragged their boat down to the water, wondering what George was doing. All kinds of crashing sounds came from the motor-boat!

'George, George! Buck up! The men are out!' Julian yelled suddenly. He could see the three men running down to the cove from the castle.

George leapt out of the motor-boat and ran towards the others. The men were hard on her heels. The others watched anxiously. It looked as

though the men would catch George before she could get into the rowing-boat!

If you think the men catch George, go to **293**. *If you think she gets away, go to* **273**.

289

'Well,' said Julian, 'we really haven't any time to lose. With any luck they'll be so interested in our story that they won't notice Timmy!'

They made their way to Kirrin Cottage at top speed. Aunt Fanny was gardening. She stared in surprise to see the hurrying children.

'Why,' she said, 'I thought you weren't coming back until tomorrow or the next day! Has anything happened?'

There was a chorus of voices.

'Aunt Fanny, where's Uncle Quentin? We have something important to tell him!'

'Mother, we've had such an adventure!'

'Aunt Fanny, we've an awful lot to tell you. We really have!'

Aunt Fanny looked at the untidy children in amazement.

'Whatever has happened?' she said. Then she called: 'Quentin! Quentin! Come here at once! The children are back, and they have something important to tell us!'

Go to **300**.

'I think we should tell him some really splendid lies,' said George, her eyes shining. 'Let's see how much we can fool him!'

'That's a jolly good idea!' exclaimed Dick.

'*Ahoy there!*' shouted the man for the third time. 'Have you come from that island over there?'

'No, we haven't!' called George.

'Did you row past it? Was there a motor-boat moored there? Did you see any men on the shore?' the man asked.

'We rowed past the island,' shouted George, 'but we didn't see a boat moored there or any men!'

'Are you sure you didn't see a boat?' yelled the man, sounding suspicious.

'No!' called George. 'Not a sign of one!'

Go to **295**.

'Oh please, Uncle Quentin, do believe us!' said Dick.

But Uncle Quentin had decided that it was all a lot of nonsense. He went back to his study.

Suddenly Anne burst into tears.

'Aunt Fanny, Aunt Fanny, it's all true!' she sobbed. 'Uncle Quentin is horrid not to believe us. Oh Aunt Fanny, the man had a revolver – and he made Julian and George prisoners in the dungeons – and Dick had to climb down the well to rescue them. And George smashed up their motor-boat to stop them escaping!'

Aunt Fanny looked at Anne's tear-stained face and the solemn faces of the others, and realised that something important really had happened.

'Wait a minute,' she said to the children, and hurried into the house to find Uncle Quentin.

Go to **287**.

292

'I shouldn't risk taking Timmy home,' said Dick. 'You know what grown-ups can be like! They'll probably be so cross at seeing Timmy that they won't take any notice of our story.'

'Let's tie him up to the boat while we find Aunt Fanny and Uncle Quentin,' said Julian. 'It'll be quicker than looking for Alf, and we really haven't any time to lose.'

'He won't like it,' said George doubtfully. 'He'll probably bark when I leave him.'

'Well, he'll just have to bark. Do come *on*, George,' replied Julian.

Go to **296**.

293

And then suddenly George tripped and fell flat on her face! Before she could get up again the men had pounced on her, dragging her to her feet.

'Thought you could get away, did you?' snarled one of the men. 'Thought you could just smash up our boat and escape. Well – we've got you now.'

'Hey – you lot!' Jake yelled to the other children, who were watching in horror from the boat, which they had already pushed out on to the water. 'You just come back here, or it'll be the worse for your friend!'

In Jake's hand they could see a gun – pointed at George's head!

Go to **276**.

294

If you have arrived from **303**, *score* ⌒.

'No,' said Uncle Quentin, his eyes twinkling. 'It's not fair to keep him in a kennel. A dog as brave and loyal as Timmy deserves better. You can keep him in the house.'

George was overjoyed! She flung her arms around her father's neck and hugged him as she had not done for a long time. He looked astonished, but pleased.

'Well, well,' he said, 'this is all very pleasant. Hello – is this the police already?'

It was. They had a word with Uncle Quentin, and then one stayed behind to take down the children's story in his notebook while the others went off to get a boat to the island.

Go to **301**.

'Is there anything else you'd like to know?' shouted Dick, a cheeky grin on his face.

But the man didn't reply. He turned away from the rail of the fishing-boat and disappeared into the cabin.

'I wonder if he believed you, George,' said Anne. 'If he did, with any luck he'll think the men on the island have cheated him by taking away the gold and leaving him behind. Perhaps he'll go and hunt for them!'

'No such luck,' said Julian, who was gazing behind him towards the fishing-boat. 'Look!'

A little boat was being lowered into the sea from the smack.

'I think he guessed you were lying, George, and if he goes to the island he'll be able to rescue the three men,' said Julian. 'But I don't think they'll dare to take any of the gold now that we've escaped.'

George rowed on.

Go to **278**.

George tied Timmy to the boat, and off they set for Kirrin Cottage. Timmy didn't bark; he sat and watched them sadly as they walked away. Then he had an idea!

The children were only half way to the cottage when suddenly Timmy came bounding up the path behind them, wagging his tail. Somehow he had managed to escape!

'Oh Timmy,' said George, 'you are awful. Well – I haven't got time to take you back now. You'll have to come too.'

They found Aunt Fanny in the garden.

'Why,' she said in amazement, 'I thought you weren't coming back until tomorrow or the next day. Has anything happened?'

'Mother, where's Father?' asked George. 'We've such a story to tell him!'

Aunt Fanny turned towards the house.

'Quentin! Quentin!' she called. 'The children are back, and they say they've something important to tell us!'

Go to **300**.

297

If you have arrived from **287**, *score* ◁.

George and Julian told the whole story, leaving nothing out. Aunt Fanny and Uncle Quentin listened in astonishment.

'Well,' said Uncle Quentin when they'd finished, 'you've been very clever, and brave too. I'm very proud of you all!'

'You must ring the police,' said Aunt Fanny. 'No doubt they'll be very interested in all this!'

Uncle Quentin went to telephone the police. The children sat and ate biscuits, telling their aunt a great many little details they had forgotten when telling the story before.

Suddenly there was a loud and angry bark from the garden!

Go to **302**.

298

'What?' asked George in surprise.

'You can ask to go to the same boarding school as I go to,' said Anne. 'It's such a lovely one – and we're allowed to keep pets, so Timmy could come too!'

'Gracious! Well, I'll go then. If I can have Timmy, that would be simply wonderful!' said George happily.

'You'd better go back to your own bedroom now, boys,' said Aunt Fanny, appearing at the doorway. 'You should all have pleasant dreams tonight!'

Go to **305**.

299

A broad grin spread over Uncle Quentin's face. 'My solicitor says that the ingots definitely belong to us!'

'Oh Father!' cried George. 'There are hundreds of them. We shall be rich, now, shan't we?'

'Yes,' said her father. 'We shall be rich, and I shall be able to give you and your mother all the things I've longed to give you for so many years and couldn't. I've worked hard enough for you, but it's not the kind of work that brings in a lot of money, and I've become irritable and bad-tempered. But now you can have anything you want!'

'Well,' said George, 'there's one thing I'd like more than anything else in the world, and it won't cost you a penny.'

'And what is that?' asked her father.

Just then Timmy's big hairy head came around the door and looked at them all.

'That's what I'd like most,' said George. 'Timmy!'

Her father frowned. 'But last time he was very disobedient, chewing up shoes and books and things, and his barking nearly drove me mad!'

'Couldn't I keep him in a kennel in the garden?' pleaded George.

If you think Uncle Quentin says yes, go to **303**. *If you think he says no, go to* **294**.

300

If you have arrived from **296**, *score* ⌢.

Uncle Quentin appeared, looking rather cross

because he was in the middle of his work. 'What's the matter?' he asked.

'Uncle, it's about Kirrin Island,' said Julian. 'Do you know why those men wanted to buy the island and the castle? Not because they really wanted to build a hotel or anything like that – but because they knew the lost gold was hidden there!'

'What nonsense are you talking?' said his uncle.

'It isn't nonsense, Father!' said George. 'The map of the castle was in that box you sold – and on the map was shown where the ingots were hidden by my great-great-great-grandfather!'

'I don't believe a word of it!' said Uncle Quentin, and he turned to go back to his study.

'Oh Father, how can we convince you?' cried George. 'Please listen!'

Uncle Quentin hesitated.

If you think Uncle Quentin decides to listen, go to **304**. *If you think he decides it's all nonsense, go to* **291**.

301

The men had gone! The boat from the fishing-smack had taken them away. The motor-boat was still there, quite unusable!

The police brought back some of the ingots to show Uncle Quentin. They had sealed the door of the dungeon so that no one else could get in until they were ready to fetch the rest of the gold. The children were rather disappointed that the men had not been caught and taken to prison.

They were all very sleepy that night, and went to bed without any fuss. They all sat in the girls' bedroom, eating their supper.

'And to think I hated the idea of you all coming here to stay!' said George. 'Now it makes me sad to think of you going away at the end of the holidays. I shall be lonely without you all.'

'You don't have to be lonely,' said Anne suddenly. 'You can do something that will stop you being lonely ever again.'

Go to **298**.

302

George looked up.

'That's Timmy,' she said, with an anxious look at her mother. 'Alf's been keeping him for me, but he came to the island with us and was such a comfort. I expect he's hungry.'

'Well, fetch him in,' said her mother unexpectedly. 'He's quite a hero, too – we must give him a good dinner.'

George smiled with delight. She sped out of doors and went to get Timmy. He came bounding in, wagging his tail. He licked George's mother, who actually patted him!

'Good dog,' she said. 'Come on, I'll get you some dinner!'

Uncle Quentin came back a moment later, his face grave.

'I've spoken to the police,' he said, 'and to my solicitor. The police are going out to the island, and I asked my solicitor about the gold.'

Go to **299**.

303

'Well, yes,' replied her father. 'I suppose you could do that.'

'But he'll be so cold in the winter,' said Anne. It was awful to think of poor Timmy in a lonely, dark kennel while they were all inside in the warmth.

'I could build him a really super weatherproof kennel!' said Julian. 'That would keep him warm and protect him from the cold. What do you think of that, George?'

George looked at her father. She suddenly noticed that he was doing his best not to laugh. She gave a shout.

'Father! You didn't mean it, did you? You didn't mean that Timmy had to be kept outside!'

Go to **294**.

304

Then Anne burst into tears! The excitement had been too much for her, and she simply couldn't bear to think that her uncle might not believe that everything was true!

'Aunt Fanny, Aunt Fanny, it's all true!' she sobbed. 'Oh Aunt Fanny, the man had a revolver – and he made Julian and George prisoners in the dungeons – and Dick had to climb down the well to rescue them! And George smashed up their motor-boat to stop them escaping!'

Her uncle and aunt couldn't make head or tail of this, but suddenly Uncle Quentin was convinced that the matter was serious and worth looking into.

'Come indoors,' he said, 'And tell me the whole story. It sounds quite extraordinary!'

Go to **297**.

305

Four happy children snuggled down into their beds. Their wonderful adventure had come to a happy end. They had plenty of holidays still in front of them – and then George would be going to school with Anne. George had Tim for her own again, the island and castle still belonged to her, and everything was marvellous!

Will the Famous Five have more adventures together?
    Yes, of course they will!
    And perhaps YOU will be there again, too.

How many red herrings have you collected?

0–25	Very good indeed! The Famous Five must have been glad to have you with them.
26–50	Promising. Perhaps your next adventure with the Famous Five will be even more successful.
51–75	You took a long time getting there, didn't you? You'll have to do better than that to keep up with the Famous Five!
More than 75	Oh dear! Perhaps you should go back to the beginning of the story and try again.

Join the Famous Five on more of their exciting adventures in *The Famous Five And You*.

If you have enjoyed The Famous Five and You
– Search for Treasure! you can now join in the
second Famous Five and You adventure:

THE FAMOUS FIVE AND YOU –
FIND ADVENTURE

Join the Famous Five on their surprise adventure at Kirrin cottage. You might discover a map to a 'secret way' or track down some mystery thieves. *You* can choose a pathway for the Five to reveal the crooks – but will you go straight to them, or will you take a false trail along the way?

KNIGHT BOOKS

A complete list of the FAMOUS FIVE ADVENTURES *by Enid Blyton*

KNIGHT BOOKS